THE FIRST, SECOND, AND THIRD
LETTERS OF SAINT JOHN
AND THE REVELATION TO SAINT JOHN

THE IGNATIUS CATHOLIC STUDY BIBLE

REVISED STANDARD VERSION
SECOND CATHOLIC EDITION

THE FIRST, SECOND, AND THIRD LETTERS OF SAINT JOHN AND THE REVELATION TO SAINT JOHN

With Introduction, Commentary, and Notes

by

Scott Hahn and Curtis Mitch

and

with Study Questions by

Dennis Walters

IGNATIUS PRESS   SAN FRANCISCO

Published with ecclesiastical approval.

Original RSV Bible text:
Nihil obstat: Thomas Hanlon, S.T.L., L.S.S., Ph.L.
Imprimatur: + Peter W. Bartholome, D.D.
Bishop of Saint Cloud, Minnesota
May 11, 1966

Introduction, commentaries, and notes:
Nihil obstat: Rev. Msgr. J. Warren Holleran, S.T.D.
Imprimatur: + Most Reverend George Niederauer
Archbishop of San Francisco
February 24, 2009

This *nihil obstat* and *imprimatur* are official declarations that a book or pamphlet is free of doctrinal or moral error. No implication is contained therein that those who have granted the *nihil obstat* and *imprimatur* agree with the contents, opinions, or statements expressed.

Second Catholic Edition approved by the
National Council of the Churches of Christ in the USA

Cover art:
Giovanni Francesco Guercino (1591–1666)
John the Evangelist
Bildarchiv Preussischer Kulturbesitz / Art Resource, N.Y.

Cover design by Riz Boncan Marsella

Printed in the United States of America ∞

CONTENTS

INTRODUCTION TO
THE IGNATIUS CATHOLIC STUDY BIBLE

by Scott Hahn, Ph.D.

You are approaching the "word of God". This is the title Christians most commonly give to the Bible, and the expression is rich in meaning. It is also the title given to the Second Person of the Blessed Trinity, God the Son. For Jesus Christ became flesh for our salvation, and "the name by which he is called is The Word of God" (Rev 19:13; cf. Jn 1:14).

The word of God is Scripture. The Word of God is Jesus. This close association between God's *written* word and his *eternal* Word is intentional and has been the custom of the Church since the first generation. "All Sacred Scripture is but one book, and this one book is Christ, 'because all divine Scripture speaks of Christ, and all divine Scripture is fulfilled in Christ'[1]" (CCC 134). This does not mean that the Scriptures are divine in the same way that Jesus is divine. They are, rather, divinely inspired and, as such, are unique in world literature, just as the Incarnation of the eternal Word is unique in human history.

Yet we can say that the inspired word resembles the incarnate Word in several important ways. Jesus Christ is the Word of God incarnate. In his humanity, he is like us in all things, except for sin. As a work of man, the Bible is like any other book, except without error. Both Christ and Scripture, says the Second Vatican Council, are given "for the sake of our salvation" (*Dei Verbum* 11), and both give us God's definitive revelation of himself. We cannot, therefore, conceive of one without the other: the Bible without Jesus, or Jesus without the Bible. Each is the interpretive key to the other. And because Christ is the subject of all the Scriptures, St. Jerome insists, "Ignorance of the Scriptures is ignorance of Christ"[2] (CCC 133).

When we approach the Bible, then, we approach Jesus, the Word of God; and in order to encounter Jesus, we must approach him in a prayerful study of the inspired word of God, the Sacred Scriptures.

Inspiration and Inerrancy The Catholic Church makes mighty claims for the Bible, and our acceptance of those claims is essential if we are to read the Scriptures and apply them to our lives as the Church intends. So it is not enough merely to nod at words like "inspired", "unique", or "inerrant". We have to understand what the Church means by these terms, and we have to make that understanding our own. After all, what we believe about the Bible will inevitably influence the way we read the Bible. The way we read the Bible, in turn, will determine what we "get out" of its sacred pages.

These principles hold true no matter what we read: a news report, a search warrant, an advertisement, a paycheck, a doctor's prescription, an eviction notice. How (or whether) we read these things depends largely upon our preconceived notions about the reliability and authority of their sources—and the potential they have for affecting our lives. In some cases, to misunderstand a document's authority can lead to dire consequences. In others, it can keep us from enjoying rewards that are rightfully ours. In the case of the Bible, both the rewards and the consequences involved take on an ultimate value.

What does the Church mean, then, when she affirms the words of St. Paul: "All Scripture is inspired by God" (2 Tim 3:16)? Since the term "inspired" in this passage could be translated "God-breathed", it follows that God breathed forth his word in the Scriptures as you and I breathe forth air when we speak. This means that God is the primary author of the Bible. He certainly employed human authors in this task as well, but he did not merely assist them while they wrote or subsequently approve what they had written. God the Holy Spirit is the *principal* author of Scripture, while the human writers are *instrumental* authors. These human authors freely wrote everything, and only those things, that God wanted: the word of God in the very words of God. This miracle of dual authorship extends to the whole of Scripture, and to every one of its parts, so that whatever the human authors affirm, God likewise affirms through their words.

The principle of biblical inerrancy follows logically from this principle of divine authorship. After all, God cannot lie, and he cannot make mistakes. Since the Bible is divinely inspired, it must be without error in everything that its divine and human authors affirm to be true. This means that biblical inerrancy is a mystery even broader in scope than infallibility, which guarantees for us that the Church will always teach the truth concerning faith and morals. Of course the mantle of inerrancy likewise covers faith and morals, but it extends even farther to ensure that all the facts and events of salvation history are accurately presented for us in the Scriptures. Inerrancy is our guarantee that the words and deeds of God found in the Bible are unified and true, declaring with one voice the wonders of his saving love.

---

[1] Hugh of St. Victor, *De arca Noe* 2, 8: PL 176, 642: cf. ibid. 2, 9: PL 176, 642–43.
[2] *DV* 25; cf. Phil 3:8 and St. Jerome, *Commentariorum in Isaiam libri xviii*, prol.: PL 24, 17b.

The guarantee of inerrancy does not mean, however, that the Bible is an all-purpose encyclopedia of information covering every field of study. The Bible is not, for example, a textbook in the empirical sciences, and it should not be treated as one. When biblical authors relate facts of the natural order, we can be sure they are speaking in a purely descriptive and "phenomenological" way, according to the way things appeared to their senses.

Biblical Authority   Implicit in these doctrines is God's desire to make himself known to the world and to enter a loving relationship with every man, woman, and child he has created. God gave us the Scriptures not just to inform or motivate us; more than anything he wants to save us. This higher purpose underlies every page of the Bible, indeed every word of it.

In order to reveal himself, God used what theologians call "accommodation". Sometimes the Lord stoops down to communicate by "condescension"—that is, he speaks as humans speak, as if he had the same passions and weakness that we do (for example, God says he was "sorry" that he made man in Genesis 6:6). Other times he communicates by "elevation"—that is, by endowing human words with divine power (for example, through the prophets). The numerous examples of divine accommodation in the Bible are an expression of God's wise and fatherly ways. For a sensitive father can speak with his children either by condescension, as in baby talk, or by elevation, by bringing a child's understanding up to a more mature level.

God's word is thus saving, fatherly, and personal. Because it speaks directly to us, we must never be indifferent to its content; after all, the word of God is at once the object, cause, and support of our faith. It is, in fact, a test of our faith, since we see in the Scriptures only what faith disposes us to see. If we believe what the Church believes, we will see in Scripture the saving, inerrant, and divinely authored revelation of the Father. If we believe otherwise, we see another book altogether.

This test applies not only to rank-and-file believers but also to the Church's theologians and hierarchy, and even the Magisterium. Vatican II has stressed in recent times that Scripture must be "the very soul of sacred theology" (*Dei Verbum* 24). As Joseph Cardinal Ratzinger, Pope Benedict XVI echoed this powerful teaching with his own, insisting that, "The *normative theologians* are the authors of Holy Scripture" (emphasis added). He reminded us that Scripture and the Church's dogmatic teaching are tied tightly together, to the point of being inseparable: "Dogma is by definition nothing other than an interpretation of Scripture." The defined dogmas of our faith, then, encapsulate the Church's infallible interpretation of Scripture, and theology is a further reflection upon that work.

The Senses of Scripture   Because the Bible has both divine and human authors, we are required to master a different sort of reading than we are used to. First, we must read Scripture according to its *literal* sense, as we read any other human literature. At this initial stage, we strive to discover the meaning of the words and expressions used by the biblical writers as they were understood in their original setting and by their original recipients. This means, among other things, that we do not interpret everything we read "literalistically", as though Scripture never speaks in a figurative or symbolic way (it often does!). Rather, we read it according to the rules that govern its different literary forms of writing, depending on whether we are reading a narrative, a poem, a letter, a parable, or an apocalyptic vision. The Church calls us to read the divine books in this way to ensure that we understand what the human authors were laboring to explain to God's people.

The literal sense, however, is not the only sense of Scripture, since we interpret its sacred pages according to the *spiritual* senses as well. In this way, we search out what the Holy Spirit is trying to tell us, beyond even what the human authors have consciously asserted. Whereas the literal sense of Scripture describes a historical reality—a fact, precept, or event—the spiritual senses disclose deeper mysteries revealed through the historical realities. What the soul is to the body, the spiritual senses are to the literal. You can distinguish them; but if you try to separate them, death immediately follows. St. Paul was the first to insist upon this and warn of its consequences: "God . . . has qualified us to be ministers of a new covenant, not in a written code but in the Spirit; for the written code kills, but the Spirit gives life" (2 Cor 3:5–6).

Catholic tradition recognizes three spiritual senses that stand upon the foundation of the literal sense of Scripture (see CCC 115). **(1)** The first is the *allegorical* sense, which unveils the spiritual and prophetic meaning of biblical history. Allegorical interpretations thus reveal how persons, events, and institutions of Scripture can point beyond themselves toward greater mysteries yet to come (OT), or display the fruits of mysteries already revealed (NT). Christians have often read the Old Testament in this way to discover how the mystery of Christ in the New Covenant was once hidden in the Old, and how the full significance of the Old Covenant was finally made manifest in the New. Allegorical significance is likewise latent in the New Testament, especially in the life and deeds of Jesus recorded in the Gospels. Because Christ is the Head of the Church and the source of her spiritual life, what was accomplished in Christ the Head during his earthly life prefigures what he continually produces in his members through grace. The allegorical sense builds up the virtue of faith. **(2)** The second is the *tropological* or *moral* sense, which reveals how the actions of God's people in the Old Testament and the life of Jesus in the New Testament prompt us to form virtuous habits in our own lives. It therefore draws from Scripture warnings against sin and vice, as well as inspirations to pursue holiness and purity. The moral sense is intended to build up the virtue of charity. **(3)** The third is the *anagogical* sense, which points upward to heavenly glory. It shows us how countless events in the Bible prefigure our final union with God in eternity, and how things that are "seen" on earth are figures of things "unseen" in heaven. Because the anagogical sense leads us to contemplate our destiny, it is meant to build up the virtue of hope. Together with the literal sense, then, these spiritual senses draw out the fullness of what God wants to give us through his Word and as such comprise what ancient tradition has called the "full sense" of Sacred Scripture.

All of this means that the deeds and events of the Bible are charged with meaning beyond what is immediately apparent to the reader. In essence, that meaning is Jesus Christ and the salvation he died to give us. This is especially true of the books of the New Testament, which proclaim Jesus explicitly; but it is also true of the Old Testament, which speaks of Jesus in more hidden and symbolic ways. The human authors of the Old Testament told us as much as they were able, but they could not clearly discern the shape of all future events standing at such a distance. It is the Bible's divine Author, the Holy Spirit, who could and did foretell the saving work of Christ, from the first page of the Book of Genesis onward.

The New Testament did not, therefore, abolish the Old. Rather, the New fulfilled the Old, and in doing so, it lifted the veil that kept hidden the face of the Lord's bride. Once the veil is removed, we suddenly see the world of the Old Covenant charged with grandeur. Water, fire, clouds, gardens, trees, hills, doves, lambs—all of these things are memorable details in the history and poetry of Israel. But now, seen in the light of Jesus Christ, they are much more. For the Christian with eyes to see, water symbolizes the saving power of Baptism; fire, the Holy Spirit; the spotless lamb, Christ crucified; Jerusalem, the city of heavenly glory.

The spiritual reading of Scripture is nothing new. Indeed the very first Christians read the Bible this way. St. Paul describes Adam as a "type" that prefigured Jesus Christ (Rom 5:14). A "type" is a real person, place, thing, or event in the Old Testament that foreshadows something greater in the New. From this term we get the word "typology", referring to the study of how the Old Testament prefigures Christ (CCC 128–30). Elsewhere St. Paul draws deeper meanings out of the story of Abraham's sons, declaring, "This is an allegory" (Gal 4:24). He is not suggesting that these events of the distant past never really happened; he is saying that the events both happened *and* signified something more glorious yet to come.

The New Testament later describes the Tabernacle of ancient Israel as "a copy and shadow of the heavenly sanctuary" (Heb 8:5) and the Mosaic Law as a "shadow of the good things to come" (Heb 10:1). St. Peter, in turn, notes that Noah and his family were "saved through water" in a way that "corresponds" to sacramental Baptism, which "now saves you" (1 Pet 3:20–21). Interestingly, the expression that is translated "corresponds" in this verse is a Greek term that denotes the fulfillment or counterpart of an ancient "type".

We need not look to the apostles, however, to justify a spiritual reading of the Bible. After all, Jesus himself read the Old Testament this way. He referred to Jonah (Mt 12:39), Solomon (Mt 12:42), the Temple (Jn 2:19), and the brazen serpent (Jn 3:14) as "signs" that pointed forward to him. We see in Luke's Gospel, as Christ comforted the disciples on the road to Emmaus, that "beginning with Moses and all the prophets, he interpreted to them in all the Scriptures the things concerning himself" (Lk 24:27). It was precisely this extensive spiritual interpretation of the Old Testament that made such an impact on these once-discouraged travelers, causing their hearts to "burn" within them (Lk 24:32).

Criteria for Biblical Interpretation   We too must learn to discern the "full sense" of Scripture as it includes both the literal and spiritual senses together. Still, this does not mean we should "read into" the Bible meanings that are not really there. Spiritual exegesis is not an unrestrained flight of the imagination. Rather, it is a sacred science that proceeds according to certain principles and stands accountable to sacred tradition, the Magisterium, and the wider community of biblical interpreters (both living and deceased).

In searching out the full sense of a text, we should always avoid the extreme tendency to "over-spiritualize" in a way that minimizes or denies the Bible's literal truth. St. Thomas Aquinas was well aware of this danger and asserted that "all other senses of Sacred Scripture are based on the literal" (*STh* I, 1, 10, *ad* 1, quoted in CCC 116). On the other hand, we should never confine the meaning of a text to the literal, intended sense of its human author, as if the divine Author did not intend the passage to be read in the light of Christ's coming.

Fortunately the Church has given us guidelines in our study of Scripture. The unique character and divine authorship of the Bible calls us to read it "in the Spirit" (*Dei Verbum* 12). Vatican II outlines this teaching in a practical way by directing us to read the Scriptures according to three specific criteria:

1. We must "[b]e especially attentive 'to the content and unity of the whole Scripture'" (CCC 112).

2. We must "[r]ead the Scripture within 'the living Tradition of the whole Church' " (CCC 113).

3. We must "[b]e attentive to the analogy of faith" (CCC 114; cf. Rom 12:6).

These criteria protect us from many of the dangers that ensnare readers of the Bible, from the newest inquirer to the most prestigious scholar. Reading Scripture out of context is one such pitfall, and probably the one most difficult to avoid. A memorable cartoon from the 1950s shows a young man poring over the pages of the Bible. He says to his sister: "Don't bother me now; I'm trying to find a Scripture verse to back up one of my preconceived notions." No doubt a biblical text pried from its context can be twisted to say something very different from what its author actually intended.

The Church's criteria guide us here by defining what constitutes the authentic "context" of a given biblical passage. The first criterion directs us to the literary context of every verse, including not only the words and paragraphs that surround it, but also the entire corpus of the biblical author's writings and, indeed, the span of the entire Bible. The *complete* literary context of any Scripture verse includes every text from Genesis to Revelation—because the Bible is a unified book, not just a library of different books. When the Church canonized the Book of Revelation, for example, she recognized it to be incomprehensible apart from the wider context of the entire Bible.

The second criterion places the Bible firmly within the context of a community that treasures a "living tradition". That community is the People of God down through the ages. Christians lived out their faith for well over a millennium before the printing press was invented. For centuries, few believers owned copies of the Gospels, and few people could read anyway. Yet they absorbed the gospel—through the sermons of their bishops and clergy, through prayer and meditation, through Christian art, through liturgical celebrations, and through oral tradition. These were expressions of the one "living tradition", a culture of living faith that stretches from ancient Israel to the contemporary Church. For the early Christians, the gospel could not be understood apart from that tradition. So it is with us. Reverence for the Church's tradition is what protects us from any sort of chronological or cultural provincialism, such as scholarly fads that arise and carry away a generation of interpreters before being dismissed by the next generation.

The third criterion places scriptural texts within the framework of faith. If we believe that the Scriptures are divinely inspired, we must also believe them to be internally coherent and consistent with all the doctrines that Christians believe. Remember, the Church's dogmas (such as the Real Presence, the papacy, the Immaculate Conception) are not something *added* to Scripture, but are the Church's infallible interpretation *of* Scripture.

Using This Study Guide   This volume is designed to lead the reader through Scripture according to the Church's guidelines—faithful to the canon, to the tradition, and to the creeds. The Church's interpretive principles have thus shaped the component parts of this book, and they are designed to make the reader's study as effective and rewarding as possible.

Introductions: We have introduced the biblical book with an essay covering issues such as authorship, date of composition, purpose, and leading themes. This background information will assist readers to approach and understand the text on its own terms.

Annotations: The basic notes at the bottom of every page help the user to read the Scriptures with understanding. They by no means exhaust the meaning of the sacred text but provide background material to help the reader make sense of what he reads. Often these notes make explicit what the sacred writers assumed or held to be implicit. They also provide scores of historical, cultural, geographical, and theological information pertinent to the inspired narratives—information that can help the reader bridge the distance between the biblical world and his own.

Cross-References: Between the biblical text at the top of each page and the annotations at the bottom, numerous references are listed to point readers to other scriptural passages related to the one being studied. This follow-up is an essential part of any serious study. It is also an excellent way to discover how the content of Scripture "hangs together" in a providential unity. Along with biblical cross-references, the annotations refer to select paragraphs from the *Catechism of the Catholic Church*. These are not doctrinal "proof texts" but are designed to help the reader interpret the Bible in accordance with the mind of the Church. The *Catechism* references listed either handle the biblical text directly or treat a broader doctrinal theme that sheds significant light on that text.

Topical Essays, Word Studies, Charts: These features bring readers to a deeper understanding of select details. The *topical essays* take up major themes and explain them more thoroughly and theologically than the annotations, often relating them to the doctrines of the Church. Occasionally the annotations are supplemented by *word studies* that put readers in touch with the ancient languages of Scripture. These should help readers to understand better and appreciate the inspired terminology that runs throughout the sacred books. Also included are various *charts* that summarize biblical information "at a glance".

Icon Annotations: Three distinctive icons are

interspersed throughout the annotations, each one corresponding to one of the Church's three criteria for biblical interpretation. Bullets indicate the passage or passages to which these icons apply.

Notes marked by the book icon relate to the "content and unity" of Scripture, showing how particular passages of the Old Testament illuminate the mysteries of the New. Much of the information in these notes explains the original context of the citations and indicates how and why this has a direct bearing on Christ or the Church. Through these notes, the reader can develop a sensitivity to the beauty and unity of God's saving plan as it stretches across both Testaments.

Notes marked by the dove icon examine particular passages in light of the Church's "living tradition". Because the Holy Spirit both guides the Magisterium and inspires the spiritual senses of Scripture, these annotations supply information along both of these lines. On the one hand, they refer to the Church's doctrinal teaching as presented by various popes, creeds, and ecumenical councils; on the other, they draw from (and paraphrase) the spiritual interpretations of various Fathers, Doctors, and saints.

Notes marked by the keys icon pertain to the "analogy of faith". Here we spell out how the mysteries of our faith "unlock" and explain one another. This type of comparison between Christian beliefs displays the coherence and unity of defined dogmas, which are the Church's infallible interpretations of Scripture.

Putting It All in Perspective Perhaps the most important context of all we have saved for last: the interior life of the individual reader. What we get out of the Bible will largely depend on how we approach the Bible. Unless we are living a sustained and disciplined life of prayer, we will never have the reverence, the profound humility, or the grace we need to see the Scriptures for what they really are.

You are approaching the "word of God". But for thousands of years, since before he knit you in your mother's womb, the Word of God has been approaching you.

One Final Note. The volume you hold in your hands is only a small part of a much larger work still in production. Study helps similar to those printed in this booklet are being prepared for *all* the books of the Bible and will appear gradually as they are finished. Our ultimate goal is to publish a single, one-volume Study Bible that will include the entire text of Scripture, along with all the annotations, charts, cross-references, maps, and other features found in the following pages. Individual booklets will be published in the meantime, with the hope that God's people can begin to benefit from this labor before its full completion.

We have included a long list of Study Questions in the back to make this format as useful as possible, not only for individual study but for group settings and discussions as well. The questions are designed to help readers both "understand" the Bible and "apply" it to their lives. We pray that God will make use of our efforts and yours to help renew the face of the earth! «

INTRODUCTION TO
THE FIRST LETTER OF SAINT JOHN

Author The First Letter of Saint John nowhere reveals the name of its author. Twelve times the epistle purports to come from an individual ("I am writing", 2:1, 7, 8, etc.), and one passage indicates that the author was writing as a spokesman on behalf of others ("we are writing", 1:4). The earliest traditions we have about the letter identify the author as the Apostle John, son of Zebedee (Mk 3:17). This was widely accepted in early Christian times and coheres well with the author's claim to give us eyewitness testimony about Jesus (1 Jn 1:1–3). The apostolic authorship of the letter has also been supported by an extensive list of verbal, conceptual, and thematic parallels between 1 John and the Gospel of John, keeping in mind that the latter work was universally attributed to the same apostle by the Church Fathers. Despite the strength and antiquity of this tradition, voices have been raised in modern times that call into question the apostolic authorship of 1 John. A popular alternative theory attributes the letter to a contemporary of the apostle named John the "elder" or "presbyter", a figure mentioned briefly by the second-century bishop Papias of Hierapolis (quoted in Eusebius, *Ecclesiastical History* 3, 39). Not only does the author of 2 and 3 John use this exact title to introduce himself to readers (2 Jn 1; 3 Jn 1), but the activity of another noteworthy John in first-century Asia Minor could explain how the name "John" came to be attached to the letter in the first place, even if subsequent generations mistook it to mean the apostle. Scholars of this opinion thus do not account for the many parallels between 1 John and the Gospel of John in the traditional way. Some concede that both works came from the hand of the same writer, but they identify this figure as someone other than the Apostle John. Others ascribe the Gospel and the epistle to two different authors and explain the similarities between them in terms of stylistic and theological influence.

In the end, the question of authorship cannot be decided conclusively. The issue is one of probability rather than provability. That said, the tradition of apostolic authorship more adequately explains the evidence than existing theories of non-apostolic authorship. Not only does early Christian testimony weigh in favor of this position, but alternative views generally lack sufficient support to overturn the tradition. For instance, it would be quite natural for the Apostle John to describe his personal encounters with Christ in the terms given in 1:1–3. However, there is no evidence to indicate that John the Elder was an eyewitness to the historical ministry of Jesus in Palestine. Of course, he could have been, but no testimony to this effect survives from antiquity. Likewise, one has to account for the preservation and eventual canonization of this letter among the writings of the New Testament. Again, it is within the realm of possibility that someone other than John the Apostle could have written 1 John; but how was its authority so readily granted in the ancient Church if its author was a non-apostle whose identity was so soon forgotten? The question has force when we consider that no rival tradition circulated in early Christianity that attributed the letter to anyone other than the apostle. So too, the testimony of Papias fails to indicate that John the Elder had ever been known as an author, much less the author of a New Testament book. On the basis of historical probability, then, it remains likely that 1 John is an authentic writing of the Apostle John.

Date Scholars tend to date 1 John after the publication of the Gospel of John. Admittedly, the evidence for this order of composition is slight, but most are inclined to think that the epistle reflects historical circumstances that arose slightly later than those that prompted the writing of the Gospel. The widespread belief that John's Gospel was written in the 90s of the first century has thus resulted in the common view that 1 John was composed around A.D. 100. Of course, an earlier date for the Gospel could mean an earlier date for 1 John as well, but support for this remains inconclusive. See introduction to the Gospel of John: *Date*.

Destination The author never identifies his readers or their location. The dominant tradition is that John eventually left the assembly of apostles in Jerusalem and made his way to Ephesus in Asia Minor, where he spent the rest of his days overseeing the churches in the region. Scholars who accept this tradition infer that John is addressing members of his flock living in Ephesus and its environs. The sense running throughout the letter that John is personally acquainted with his readers and their situation makes this a strong possibility (2:1, 12–14; 3:11).

Purpose The letter aims to strengthen believers threatened by a heretical group that broke away from their community (2:19). These individuals—whom John calls antichrists, liars, deceivers, and false prophets—denied that Jesus was "the Christ" (2:22; 5:1) and "the Son of God" (2:23; 5:5) who had truly "come in the flesh" (4:2). Attempts have been made to identify these apostates with various heretical groups that cropped up in the second century, such as the *Docetists*, who denied the reality of Christ's humanity, the *Gnostics*, who had a deep aversion to the physical and material element of man, or the *Cerinthians*, who claimed that the Divine Person of Christ descended on the man Jesus at his Baptism but withdrew from him just before the Passion. Others see them as former converts from *Judaism* who became increasingly troubled by the doctrine of the Incarnation and the messianic title that Christians gave to Jesus. Whatever the background of these opponents, John wanted to expose their propaganda as contrary to the apostolic faith handed down since the beginning.

Themes and Characteristics The formalities of correspondence that usually characterize ancient letters are absent from 1 John. That is, it never identifies the sender or the recipients, nor does it contain a personal greeting or farewell. Perhaps more than any other New Testament book, 1 John resembles a short catechetical treatise. Still, the work appears to be more spontaneous than systematic in its presentation of Christian doctrine, and its warm, pastoral tone has notable affinities with the canonical letters of Peter, Paul, and James. We might think of it more as a pastoral exhortation than a formal letter. Nevertheless, in terms of literary form, it is undeniable that 1 John

is something unique, something that resists a neat and tidy classification among other works of its kind. Be that as it may, longstanding tradition counts 1 John as one of the seven "Catholic Epistles" of the New Testament.

The content of the letter focuses on authentic fellowship with God. Faced with innovators who broke away from Christian orthodoxy, John's readers need assurance that they have embraced the true gospel that comes from the apostles. He therefore stresses that they—and not other rival groups—possess what was passed down from "the beginning" (1:1; 2:7, 13, 24; 3:11). They are the ones whose faith is victorious (5:4) and whose fellowship with God is certain (1:3; 3:24), provided they walk in the light (1:7), confess their sins (1:9), keep the commandments (2:3), and love one another in word and deed (3:18). The difference between true and false believers emerges as John divides the world into light and darkness (1:5), truth and error (4:6), love and hate (2:10–11), life and death (3:14), Christ and the antichrists (2:22). The line that runs between these contrasts is also the line that distinguishes children of God from the children of Satan (3:10). At the height of all these reflections stands the triune God, who is light, life, and love (1:5; 4:8; 5:11). The fellowship that believers enjoy with the Father rests on the grace of divine life that is given us by the Son (5:12) and abides in us by the indwelling of the Spirit (3:24). This gives John the boldness to insist that we are truly "children of God" (3:1) born of the Father (3:9) for eternal life (5:13). «

OUTLINE OF THE FIRST LETTER OF SAINT JOHN

1. **Prologue (1:1–4)**

2. **Living in the Light (1:5—3:10)**
   A. Fellowship with God and One Another (1:5—2:6)
   B. Loving God and One Another (2:7–17)
   C. Exposing the Antichrist (2:18–29)
   D. Revealing the Children of God (3:1–10)

3. **Living in Love (3:11—5:12)**
   A. Loving the Brethren (3:11–24)
   B. Discerning the Spirits (4:1–6)
   C. God Is Love (4:7–21)
   D. Faith and Life in God the Son (5:1–12)

4. **Conclusion (5:13–21)**

THE FIRST LETTER OF
SAINT JOHN

The Word of Life

1 That which was from the beginning, which we have heard, which we have seen with our eyes, which we have looked upon and touched with our hands, concerning the word of life—²the life was made manifest, and we saw it, and testify to it, and proclaim to you the eternal life which was with the Father and was made manifest to us—³that which we have seen and heard we proclaim also to you, so that you may have fellowship with us; and our fellowship is with the Father and with his Son Jesus Christ. ⁴And we are writing this that our ᵃ joy may be complete.

God Is Light

5 This is the message we have heard from him and proclaim to you, that God is light and in him is no darkness at all. ⁶If we say we have fellowship with him while we walk in darkness, we lie and do not live according to the truth; ⁷but if we walk in the light, as he is in the light, we have fellowship with one another, and the blood of Jesus his Son cleanses us from all sin. ⁸If we say we have no sin, we deceive ourselves, and the truth is not in us. ⁹If we confess our sins, he is faithful and just, and will forgive our sins and cleanse us from all unrighteousness. ¹⁰If we say we have not sinned, we make him a liar, and his word is not in us.

Christ Is Our Advocate

2 My little children, I am writing this to you so that you may not sin; but if any one does sin, we have an advocate with the Father, Jesus Christ

---

1:1–2: Lk 24:39; Jn 1:1; 4:14; 15:27; 20:20, 25; Acts 4:20; 1 Jn 2:13.   **1:4:** Jn 15:11; 2 Jn 12.   **1:5:** 1 Jn 3:11.
1:6–8: Jn 3:21; 1 Jn 2:4, 11.   **1:7:** Rev 1:5.   **1:10:** 1 Jn 5:10.   **2:1:** Jn 14:16.

1:1–4 The prologue gives witness to the mystery of the Incarnation. John speaks for all the apostles ("we") when he testifies that Jesus is the **life** and **Son** of God who manifested himself in a visible, audible, and tangible way when he came in the flesh as a man (4:2). ● John describes the Incarnation in terms applicable to the sacraments of the Church. Through these liturgical signs and actions, Christ continues to give his life to the world in ways perceptible by our senses (CCC 1145–52). This is particularly true of the Eucharist, which gives us the human "flesh" (1 Jn 4:2) and "blood" (5:6) of Jesus in its risen and glorified state.

1:1 the beginning: I.e., when the Christian message first reached the original readers (2:7, 24; 3:11). There is also an allusion to "the beginning" mentioned in Jn 1:1, where the reference points back to the dawn of creation, when God brought all things into being through his divine Son (1 Jn 2:13–14; 3:8). **the word of life:** The good news of the gospel. Its focus is the personal "Word" of the Father, Jesus Christ (Jn 1:1; Rev 19:13). See word study: *Word* at Jn 1:1.

1:2 with the Father: Christ embodies the eternal life (5:11) that he shares with the Father in his divinity (Jn 5:26). This means that Christ himself is "true God" (1 Jn 5:20; Jn 1:1) and that he reveals to us the mystery of God's inner life as a Trinity (Jn 1:18).

1:3 fellowship: The interpersonal communion that believers have with God and with one another (1:6–7). It is based on a common participation in divine life that establishes us as God's children (3:1). The apostles extend this gift to others by their preaching and sacramental ministry (1 Cor 10:16–17; CCC 425).

1:5 God is light: Means that God is infinite goodness, purity, and truth. **darkness:** Stands for all things evil and erroneous that are churned out by the devil (Jn 3:19–21). Fellowship with God is impossible unless believers live in the light—loving as God loves and staying pure from sin as God is pure (1 Jn 1:6–7). This black-and-white vision of the world is also shared by the Jewish authors of the Dead Sea Scrolls, who made similar contrasts between spiritual realities in terms of light and darkness.

1:8 we have no sin: An outrageous claim. John cautions readers that stubborn refusal to admit sin is a delusion and at the same time an insult to God (1:10) (CCC 827).

1:9 If we confess: John envisions, not a general admission of weakness or even sinfulness, but the confession of specific acts of wrongdoing (Ps 32:3–5). God, for his part, is eager to show mercy to the contrite spirit (Ps 51:17). Contrary to the teaching of some, the need for repentance, confession, and forgiveness is ongoing throughout the Christian life; otherwise, the Lord would not urge believers to seek forgiveness on a continuing basis (Mt 6:12; Lk 11:4). Note that in biblical terms "confession" (Gk. *homologeō*) is something you do with your *lips* and not simply in the silence of your heart (Mk 1:5; Rom 10:10; Jas 5:16) (CCC 2631). ● The Church encourages the private confession of sins to God. Ordinarily, however, this should lead us to the Sacrament of Reconciliation. Jesus implies as much in Jn 20:23, where he gives the apostles his own authority to remit or retain sins according to their discretion. This discretion could not be exercised apart from knowledge of specific sins acquired by the verbal confession of sinners (CCC 1461, 2839). ● Priestly confession is not a Christian innovation but an extension and sacramental elevation of a practice long observed in Israel (Lev 5:5–6; Num 5:5–10).

2:1–6 John recognizes that sin can be a nagging problem in the lives of believers. It is not a problem without a solution, however, since Jesus Christ is our advocate (2:1), our sin-offering (2:2), and our moral example (2:6).

2:1 advocate: Refers to an "attorney" or "defense lawyer" in contemporary Greek literature. Jesus spoke of himself (Jn

---

ᵃ Other ancient authorities read *your*.

the righteous; [2]and he is the expiation for our sins, and not for ours only but also for the sins of the whole world. [3]And by this we may be sure that we know him, if we keep his commandments. [4]He who says "I know him" but disobeys his commandments is a liar, and the truth is not in him; [5]but whoever keeps his word, in him truly love for God is perfected. By this we may be sure that we are in him: [6]he who says he abides in him ought to walk in the same way in which he walked.

A New Commandment

7 Beloved, I am writing you no new commandment, but an old commandment which you had from the beginning; the old commandment is the word which you have heard. [8]Yet I am writing you a new commandment, which is true in him and in you, because [b] the darkness is passing away and the true light is already shining. [9]He who says he is in the light and hates his brother is in the darkness still. [10]He who loves his brother abides in the light, and in it [c] there is no cause for stumbling. [11]But he who hates his brother is in the darkness and walks in the darkness, and does not know where he is going, because the darkness has blinded his eyes.

12 I am writing to you, little children, because your sins are forgiven for his sake. [13]I am writing to you, fathers, because you know him who is from the beginning. I am writing to you, young men, because you have overcome the Evil One. I write to you, children, because you know the Father. [14]I write to you, fathers, because you know him who is from the beginning. I am writing to you, young men, because you are strong, and the word of God abides in you, and you have overcome the Evil One.

15 Do not love the world or the things in the world. If any one loves the world, love for the Father is not in him. [16]For all that is in the world, the lust of the flesh and the lust of the eyes and the pride of life, is not of the Father but is of the world. [17]And the world passes away, and the lust of it; but he who does the will of God abides for ever.

Warning against the Antichrist

18 Children, it is the last hour; and as you have heard that antichrist is coming, so now many antichrists have come; therefore we know that it is

---

2:2: Jn 1:29; 3:14–16; 11:51–52; 1 Jn 4:10.   **2:3:** Jn 15:10.   **2:4:** 1 Jn 1:6–8; 4:20.   **2:5:** Jn 14:21, 23; 1 Jn 5:3.   **2:6:** Jn 13:15.   **2:7:** Jn 13:34.   **2:8:** Jn 8:12.   **2:10–11:** Jn 11:9–10; 1 Jn 1:6.   **2:13:** Jn 1:1; 1 Jn 1:1.   **2:18:** 1 Jn 4:3.

14:16) and of the Spirit in this way (Jn 14:26; 15:26). Advocacy is needed before the Father when our sins prompt the devil to bring accusations against us (Rev 12:10) (CCC 519). See word study: *Counselor* at Jn 14:16.

✠ **2:2 sins of the whole world:** The redeeming work of Christ embraces all times, all places, and all peoples (Jn 1:29). Not a single individual has lived or will live for whom Christ did not die (2 Cor 5:15; CCC 605). See note on 1 Tim 2:4. ● One makes satisfaction for an offense when he offers the person offended something of equal or greater value. Christ, by suffering in a spirit of love and obedience, offered to God more than the recompense required for all the offenses of the human race. His Passion was not only sufficient but superabundant satisfaction for the world's sins (St. Thomas Aquinas, *Summa Theologiae*, III, 48, 2).

2:3 keep his commandments: The Father gives guidance to his children (3:1) for living and growing in maturity. Obedience

---

[b] Or *that*.   [c] Or *him*.

Word Study

Expiation (1 Jn 2:2)

Hilasmos (Gk.): a term that can mean "propitiation" with reference to God or "expiation" with reference to sin. The word is used only twice in the NT (1 Jn 2:2; 4:10) but is related to other biblical terms with a similar meaning (Lk 18:13; Rom 3:25; Heb 2:17). In all of these instances, the notion of removing or wiping away sin is in view. The basis for this understanding comes from the Greek OT, where *hilasmos* is a cultic term that refers to an expiatory sacrifice of atonement (Num 5:8; Ezek 44:27; 2 Mac 3:33). John interprets the death of Jesus along the same lines: the shedding of his blood on the Cross was an act of sacrifice that takes away the sins of the world (Jn 1:29; 1 Jn 1:7) (CCC 457, 614).

---

to his commandments gives us the moral certitude that we are living as true sons and daughters. In essence, this amounts to imitating Christ (2:6), who showed us how to follow the Father's commandments without exception or fault (Jn 15:10).

2:6 the same way . . . he walked: Assumes readers are familiar with the life and ministry of Jesus, probably from the Gospel of John (CCC 2470).

2:7 no new commandment: John's teaching is not a recent innovation unfamiliar to his readers. It is, rather, the commandment to love one another (2:10) that they received with the gospel and that ultimately goes back to Jesus (Jn 13:34). The point is that John's catechesis is an authentic expression of apostolic doctrine (CCC 2822). See note on Jn 13:34.

2:8 the true light: Refers to the gospel in general and to Jesus Christ in particular (Jn 1:9).

2:9 He who says . . . and hates: A believer's conduct must agree with his confession for his fellowship with God to be genuine. Faith without faithfulness is not a saving faith at all (Jas 2:14–17). See note on Jn 3:36.

2:12–14 Readers are assured that Christ's blessings have come upon them: their sins are **forgiven** (2:12), they **know** the living God (2:13–14), and they are victorious over the **Evil One** (2:13–14). It is possible that John's address to children, fathers, and young men refers, not to various age groups, but to three levels of spiritual maturity (1 Cor 3:1; Heb 5:12–14).

2:15–17 John urges readers to let go of the world and embrace the Father (4:4). Although God made (Gen 1:1) and loves the world (Jn 3:16), the human family turned against him and surrendered itself to the devil (1 Jn 5:19). Since then, the propensity of fallen man is to love the world in selfish and disordered ways—feeding his **flesh** with its pleasures, his **eyes** with its possessions, and his spirit with its **pride**. Christians are called to renounce the world, not as something evil or detestable, but as something that threatens to consume our attention and turn our affections away from God. The ascetical disciplines of prayer, fasting, and almsgiving are venerated in Jewish and Christian tradition as practical ways to express our love for God and lessen our love for the world (Tob 12:8–10; Mt 6:2–18) (CCC 377, 2514). For different meanings of the term "world" in the writings of John, see note on Jn 1:10.

2:18 the last hour: The final phase of salvation history set in motion by Christ. Paul refers to this last epoch as "the end of

---

the last hour. [19]They went out from us, but they were not of us; for if they had been of us, they would have continued with us; but they went out, that it might be plain that they all are not of us. [20]But you have been anointed by the Holy One, and you all know. [d] [21]I write to you, not because you do not know the truth, but because you know it, and know that no lie is of the truth. [22]Who is the liar but he who denies that Jesus is the Christ? This is the antichrist, he who denies the Father and the Son. [23]Any one who denies the Son does not have the Father. He who confesses the Son has the Father also. [24]Let what you heard from the beginning abide in you. If what you heard from the beginning abides in you, then you will abide in the Son and in the Father. [25]And this is what he has promised us, [e] eternal life.

26 I write this to you about those who would deceive you; [27]but the anointing which you received from him abides in you, and you have no need that any one should teach you; as his anointing teaches you about everything, and is true, and is no lie, just as it has taught you, abide in him.

Children of God

28 And now, little children, abide in him, so that when he appears we may have confidence and not shrink from him in shame at his coming. [29]If you know that he is righteous, you may be sure that every one who does right is born of him.

3 See what love the Father has given us, that we should be called children of God; and so we are. The reason why the world does not know us is that it did not know him. [2]Beloved, we are God's children now; it does not yet appear what we shall be, but we know that when he appears we shall be like him, for we shall see him as he is. [3]And every one who thus hopes in him purifies himself as he is pure.

4 Every one who commits sin is guilty of lawlessness; sin is lawlessness. [5]You know that he appeared to take away sins, and in him there is no sin. [6]Any one who abides in him does not sin; any one who sins has not seen him, nor has he known him. [7]Little children, let no one deceive you. He who

---

2:22: 2 Jn 7.   **2:23:** 1 Jn 4:15; 2 Jn 9.   **2:27:** Jn 14:26.   **2:28:** 1 Jn 4:17.   **2:29:** 1 Jn 3:7–10; 4:7.
3:1: Jn 1:12; 16:3.   **3:5:** Jn 1:29.

---

the ages" (1 Cor 10:11), just as Peter calls it "the end of the times" (1 Pet 1:20). These and similar expressions underscore the need for Christians to remain vigilant as they wait in joyful hope for the Lord's return in glory (CCC 670). **antichrist:** Or, "anti-messiah". Here the title applies to anyone who denies that Jesus is the anointed "Christ" or "Messiah" of Jewish expectation (1 Jn 2:22; 4:3; 2 Jn 7). In a restricted sense, the "Antichrist" is a blasphemous figure expected to appear at the end of days. His coming will thrust the Church into a time of persecution and set off an explosion of evil and deception in the world at large (CCC 675–77). For a description of this eschatological villain, see 2 Thess 2:3–11.

2:19 They went out: I.e., the heretical secessionists, who broke away from the Church in order to follow their corrupt ways. For John, their departure is a sure sign of their deviation from the apostolic faith. The comment at 2:26 suggests the apostates were not content simply to leave, but were making active attempts to carry others astray with them.

2:20 anointed: Refers to a special grace of the Holy Spirit, which instructs believers in the truth and alerts them to false teaching (2:26–27). There is a close relationship between confessing Jesus as the Messiah (Gk. *Christos*, 2:22) and receiving his anointing (Gk *chrisma*, 2:27), for the same Spirit who anointed Jesus (Acts 10:38) dwells in the hearts of all who are baptized in his name (Acts 2:38) (CCC 695). ● Isaiah foresaw the anointing of the Messiah, not with oil, like the prophets, priests, and kings of Israel, but with the Spirit of Yahweh (Is 61:1). The descending Spirit brings many gifts with him, including wisdom, understanding, and knowledge (Is 11:2). ● Vatican II teaches that all the faithful, clergy and laity alike, are anointed with a supernatural insight into the gospel (known in Latin as the *sensus fidei*). Graced in this way, the Church as a whole, guided by the teaching authority of the pope and bishops, will always give universal consent to the truth about Christian faith and life (*Lumen Gentium* 12) (CCC 91–93). **the Holy One:** Probably refers to Jesus (Mk 1:24; Jn 6:69), though the Father bears this title, as well (Job 6:10; Is 1:4).

2:28 confidence: Faithfulness to Christ shelters us from condemnation both now (Rom 8:1) and when he comes again to judge the world (Acts 10:42). Although individuals cannot have

absolute assurance of their final salvation, they can be certain that perseverance in faith and active charity will be approved by God (Mt 25:31–46). See word study: *Confidence* at 1 Jn 4:17.

3:1 children of God: Believers become sons and daughters of God by the grace of divine generation, which is received by faith (Jn 1:12–13) through the water and Spirit of Baptism (Jn 3:5). Those who are blessed in this way are entitled to God's love and protection (Jn 16:27; 17:15), empowered to love others as Jesus did (1 Jn 3:16–18; Jn 13:34), and encouraged to direct their hearts, hopes, and prayers to the Father through Christ (Lk 11:1–14; Jn 14:2–3). Note that believers are born of God by grace (1 Jn 2:29; 3:9; 4:7; 5:4), whereas Christ is the "only Son" of the Father by nature (4:9; Jn 1:18; 3:16). Paul implies such a distinction when he describes our sonship in Christ in terms of divine adoption (Gal 4:4–7) (CCC 460, 1692). **and so we are:** Our dignity as children of God is not in *name* only. It is the result of truly sharing in his divine *nature* (1 Jn 3:9; 2 Pet 1:4).

3:2 see him as he is: The glory that awaits believers is nothing less than a direct vision of Christ. John implies in 3:3 what Jesus states explicitly in the Beatitudes: the vision of God is a blessing reserved for those who are pure (Mt 5:8; CCC 163, 2519). See note on 1 Cor 13:12.

3:5 there is no sin: Refers to the absolute sinlessness of Jesus (Jn 8:46; Heb 4:15; 1 Pet 2:22).

3:6 does not sin: The point is not that sinless perfection is required to call oneself a Christian, but that true believers refuse to lead lives dominated by sin. Instead, they strive to break free from godless habits, and, whenever necessary, they seek God's mercy through confession (1:9; 2:1). This focus on the moral life leads John into a discussion about family likeness: the children of the devil act like the devil, while the children of God imitate the love of God (3:7–10). ● Even now we are the children of God because we possess the firstfruits of the Spirit. However, since we are not yet fully saved or renewed, we are also children of the world. This explains why we are still able to sin. Insofar as we are sons of God by the regenerating Spirit, we cannot commit sin; and yet, if we say that we have no sin, we are only deceiving ourselves (St. Augustine, *On the Merits and Remission of Sins* 2, 10).

3:7 righteous: Believers share in the righteousness of Christ as a free gift of grace (Rom 5:17). However, once established

---

[d] Other ancient authorities read *you know everything.*
[e] Other ancient authorities read *you.*

does right is righteous, as he is righteous. [8]He who commits sin is of the devil; for the devil has sinned from the beginning. The reason the Son of God appeared was to destroy the works of the devil. [9]Any one born of God does not commit sin; for God's [f] seed abides in him, and he cannot sin because he is [g] born of God. [10]By this it may be seen who are the children of God, and who are the children of the devil: whoever does not do right is not of God, nor he who does not love his brother.

Love One Another

11 For this is the message which you have heard from the beginning, that we should love one another, [12]and not be like Cain who was of the Evil One and murdered his brother. And why did he murder him? Because his own deeds were evil and his brother's righteous. [13]Do not wonder, brethren, that the world hates you. [14]We know that we have passed out of death into life, because we love the brethren. He who does not love remains in death. [15]Any one who hates his brother is a murderer, and you know that no murderer has eternal life abiding in him. [16]By this we know love, that he laid down his life for us; and we ought to lay down our lives for the brethren. [17]But if any one has the world's goods and sees his brother in need, yet closes his heart against him, how does God's love abide in him? [18]Little children, let us not love in word or speech but in deed and in truth.

19 By this we shall know that we are of the truth, and reassure our hearts before him [20]whenever our hearts condemn us; for God is greater than our hearts, and he knows everything. [21]Beloved, if our hearts do not condemn us, we have confidence before God; [22]and we receive from him whatever we ask, because we keep his commandments and do what pleases him. [23]And this is his commandment, that we should believe in the name of his Son Jesus Christ and love one another, just as he has commanded us. [24]All who keep his commandments abide in him, and he in them. And by this we know that he abides in us, by the Spirit which he has given us.

Testing the Spirits

4 Beloved, do not believe every spirit, but test the spirits to see whether they are of God; for many false prophets have gone out into the world. [2]By this you know the Spirit of God: every spirit which confesses that Jesus Christ has come in the flesh is of God, [3]and every spirit which does not confess Jesus is not of God. This is the spirit of antichrist, of which you heard that it was coming, and now it is in the world already. [4]Little children, you are of God, and have overcome them; for he

---

3:8: Jn 8:34, 44. **3:9:** 1 Jn 5:18. **3:11:** 1 Jn 1:5. **3:13:** Jn 15:18–19. **3:14:** Jn 5:24. **3:15:** Jn 8:44. **3:16:** Jn 13:1; 15:13. **3:18:** Jas 1:22. **3:21:** 1 Jn 5:14. **3:23:** Jn 6:29; 13:34; 15:17. **3:24:** 1 Jn 4:13. **4:3:** 1 Jn 2:18.

---

in grace, obedience to the gospel leads to a greater possession of righteousness (Rom 6:16) inasmuch as the Spirit enables us to fulfill the righteous demands of God's law (Rom 8:4). Scripture can thus speak of righteousness as an "unmerited" gift as well as something progressively "merited" through obedience, which is itself the work of grace.

3:12 like Cain: The only direct reference to the OT in 1 John. • The actions of Cain constitute the first example of fraternal hatred in the Bible (Gen 4:1–16). His envy of Abel mirrored the devil's envy of Adam (Wis 2:24); so the murderous act that ensued made him a child of the devil, who was a "murderer from the beginning" (Jn 8:44). John is saying that hatred among fellow Christians is on a par with homicide (1 Jn 3:15).

3:14 death into life: A transfer from one spiritual state to another (Jn 5:24). Spiritual death is a state of separation from God caused by sin (Rom 5:12; 6:23). Spiritual life, by contrast, is a state of union with God effected by the infusion of divine life into the believer (1 Jn 4:4, 9, 13, 16; 5:11–12).

3:16 lay down our lives: The supreme expression of love according to Jesus (Jn 15:13). Some are called to a *dying* martyrdom, which consists of the total surrender of human life in a generous act of love and fidelity to the faith. Everyone, however, is called to a *living* martyrdom, which involves a lifetime of sacrifice for the love and benefit of others. John's plea to help the needy with tangible assistance is one such way of giving ourselves to others (1 Jn 3:17–18) (CCC 459, 2447).

3:19–20 These verses are difficult to translate. Another possibility is: "By this we shall know that we are of the truth, and we shall persuade our hearts before him, if our hearts condemn us, that God is greater than our hearts and knows everything." The idea seems to be that Christians, despite being conscious of their shortcomings in life, can stand before God at the Judgment with confidence in the superabundance of his mercy.

3:20 condemn us: The heart that convicts a believer of sin is beating with the truth. It responds with contrition and immediately seeks forgiveness from Christ (1:9). The refusal to admit sin is a sure sign of deception and alienation from the truth (1:8) (CCC 1781). **God is greater:** God has the power to cleanse our conscience and restore our confidence to approach him prayerfully with our needs (3:22; CCC 208).

3:23 his commandment: The demands of faith and love that direct us to God (Jn 14:1) and our neighbor (Jn 15:12). **believe in the name:** I.e., believe in the Person signified by the name. Faith in the name of Jesus implies acceptance of the truth of his identity, namely, that he is "the Christ" (5:1) and "the Son of God" (5:5). The same teaching appears in the Gospel of John (e.g., Jn 1:49; 7:41; 11:27; 20:31).

4:1 test the spirits: An appeal for spiritual discernment. Readers must distinguish lying spirits, who whisper words of deceit into the ears of the false prophets, from the Holy Spirit, whose voice is heard in the teaching of the apostles (Jn 14:26; 16:13). As a practical test, John proposes that one's confession of faith—especially in Christ's Incarnation (1 Jn 4:2)—must measure up to the apostolic gospel to be genuine and true. To confess otherwise is to contradict the Spirit (1 Cor 12:3). **false prophets:** The heretics who deserted John's community (2:19). Both Jesus and the apostles warned of their arrival (Mt 24:11; 1 Tim 4:1; 2 Pet 2:1).

4:2 come in the flesh: The most serious denial of the false teachers (2 Jn 7). John makes several emphatic assertions about the physical reality of Jesus' humanity to counter this rejection (1 Jn 1:1–2; 4:14; 5:6–8; Jn 1:14). Denial of the Incarnation of Christ took many forms in Christian antiquity (CCC 465). See introduction to 1 John: *Purpose*.

4:3 spirit of antichrist: A mentality hostile to the messianic dignity of Jesus. See note on 1 Jn 2:18.

4:4 he who is in you: The indwelling Spirit, who empowers us to resist deception by the strength of the truth (3:24; 4:13). This is one way believers share in Christ's victory over the devil

---

[f] Greek *his.*
[g] Or *for the offspring of God abide in him, and they cannot sin because they are.*

who is in you is greater than he who is in the world. [5]They are of the world, therefore what they say is of the world, and the world listens to them. [6]We are of God. Whoever knows God listens to us, and he who is not of God does not listen to us. By this we know the spirit of truth and the spirit of error.

God Is Love

7 Beloved, let us love one another; for love is of God, and he who loves is born of God and knows God. [8]He who does not love does not know God; for God is love. [9]In this the love of God was made manifest among us, that God sent his only-begotten Son into the world, so that we might live through him. [10]In this is love, not that we loved God but that he loved us and sent his Son to be the expiation for our sins. [11]Beloved, if God so loved us, we also ought to love one another. [12]No man has ever seen God; if we love one another, God abides in us and his love is perfected in us.

13 By this we know that we abide in him and he in us, because he has given us of his own Spirit. [14]And we have seen and testify that the Father has sent his Son as the Savior of the world. [15]Whoever confesses that Jesus is the Son of God, God abides in him, and he in God. [16]So we know and believe the love God has for us. God is love, and he who abides in love abides in God, and God abides in him. [17]In this is love perfected with us, that we may have confidence for the day of judgment, because as he is so are we in this world. [18]There is no fear in love, but perfect love casts out fear. For fear has to do with punishment, and he who fears is not perfected in love. [19]We love, because he first loved us. [20]If any one says, "I love God," and hates his brother, he is a liar; for he who does not love his brother whom he has seen, cannot [h] love God whom he has not seen. [21]And this commandment we have from him, that he who loves God should love his brother also.

Faith Conquers the World

5 Every one who believes that Jesus is the Christ has been born of God, and every one who loves the parent loves the one begotten by him. [2]By this we know that we love the children of God, when we love God and obey his commandments. [3]For this is the love of God, that we keep his commandments. And his commandments are not burdensome. [4]For whatever is born of God overcomes the world; and this is the victory that overcomes the world, our faith. [5]Who is it that overcomes the world but he who believes that Jesus is the Son of God?

4:5: Jn 15:19. **4:6:** Jn 8:47. **4:7:** 1 Jn 2:29. **4:9:** Jn 3:16. **4:10:** Jn 15:12; 1 Jn 4:19; 2:2. **4:12:** Jn 1:18. **4:13:** 1 Jn 3:24. **4:14:** Jn 4:42; 3:17. **4:17:** 1 Jn 2:28. **4:19:** 1 Jn 4:10. **4:20:** 1 Jn 2:4. **5:1:** Jn 8:42. **5:3:** Jn 14:15; 1 Jn 2:5; 2 Jn 6. **5:4:** Jn 16:33.

(3:8), who still holds the unbelieving world captive in ignorance and error (5:19).

4:6 listens to us: I.e., to the apostles (1:3–4).

4:8 God is love: God exists as an eternal act of love, with the Father, Son, and Spirit giving themselves to one another in an everlasting embrace. This love of the Trinity, which has its eternal source in the Father, spills over into history through the sacrificial love of the Son (Rom 5:8) and the sanctifying love of the Spirit (Rom 5:5). For John, we can be sure that God lives in us if we love others as God loves—genuinely, sacrificially, unconditionally. In this way, God's trinitarian love is reflected on earth as it is in heaven (CCC 221). See note on Jn 14:31.

4:9 his only-begotten Son: The Greek can refer either to the "divine generation" of the Son or to his "uniqueness". Both senses may be intended, for neither is exclusive of the other (Jn 1:18) (CCC 444).

4:10 expiation: An atoning sacrifice for sin. See word study: *Expiation* at 1 Jn 2:2.

4:12 has ever seen God: The divine essence of God is invisible spirit (Jn 4:24). His divine love, however, is made visible in the humanity and mission of Jesus (Jn 14:9) and in the selfless charity of his followers (Jn 13:35; CCC 516). See note on Jn 1:18.

4:18 love casts out fear: The more we love God and one another, the more our ability to love increases and the closer we draw to the Source of love (4:7). Over time, the exercise of charity instills a sense of moral security that expels anxiety about our fate at the final Judgment (2:28; 4:17).

4:19 because he first loved us: The love we receive from God gives us the capacity to return his love and spread it to others. So what was *impossible* for sinners alienated from God's love is now *possible* because of God's initiative and forgiveness (4:10, 21). True love, John is saying, originates, not in the human heart, but in God (Rom 5:5) (CCC 604, 733).

5:1 Jesus is the Christ: For a confession of faith to be orthodox, it must affirm that Jesus of Nazareth is the Messiah anointed by Yahweh (2:22). The same standard applies to belief in Jesus' divine Sonship (5:5) (CCC 436, 454). See note on 1 Jn 2:18.

5:3 the love of God: Love for God is an act of the will that expresses itself in obedience to his commandments (Jn 14:15). It directs us to fulfill his law by loving one another (1 Jn 3:23) and adhering to the Ten Commandments (Rom 13:8–10).

5:4 our faith: Faith opens the way to salvation and rescues us from the sinful world. The towering importance of faith is

Word Study

Confidence (1 Jn 4:17)

Parrēsia (Gk.): means "boldness", "courage", or "outspokenness". The term is found four times in 1 John and 27 times in the rest of the NT. Often used in the context of speech, it describes words that are clear and straightforward (Jn 11:14; 16:25), as well as words that are spoken openly and publicly (Jn 7:26; Acts 28:31). In a similar way, it refers to the confidence that believers have when they approach God with their prayers (Heb 4:16; 1 Jn 5:14). The term is used several times in 1 John for the sense of security that Christians have in their relationship with God. It is not presumption, but the filial boldness of a child before his Father that allows us to live on open terms with the Lord without a servile or inordinate fear of his judgment (1 Jn 2:28; 3:21; 4:17) (CCC 2778).

---

[h] Other ancient authorities read *how can he.*

Testimony concerning the Son of God

6 This is he who came by water and blood, Jesus Christ, not with the water only but with the water and the blood. ⁷And the Spirit is the witness, because the Spirit is the truth. ⁸There are three witnesses, the Spirit, the water, and the blood; and these three agree. ⁹If we receive the testimony of men, the testimony of God is greater; for this is the testimony of God that he has borne witness to his Son. ¹⁰He who believes in the Son of God has the testimony in himself. He who does not believe God has made him a liar, because he has not believed in the testimony that God has borne to his Son. ¹¹And this is the testimony, that God gave us eternal life, and this life is in his Son. ¹²He who has the Son has life; he who has not the Son of God has not life.

Epilogue

13 I write this to you who believe in the name of the Son of God, that you may know that you have eternal life. ¹⁴And this is the confidence which we have in him, that if we ask anything according to his will he hears us. ¹⁵And if we know that he hears us in whatever we ask, we know that we have obtained the requests made of him. ¹⁶If any one sees his brother committing what is not a deadly sin, he will ask, and God[1] will give him life for those whose sin is not deadly. There is sin which is deadly; I do not say that one is to pray for that. ¹⁷All wrongdoing is sin, but there is sin which is not deadly.

18 We know that any one born of God does not sin, but He who was born of God keeps him, and the Evil One does not touch him.

19 We know that we are of God, and the whole world is in the power of the Evil One.

20 And we know that the Son of God has come and has given us understanding, to know him who is true; and we are in him who is true, in his Son Jesus Christ. This is the true God and eternal life. ²¹Little children, keep yourselves from idols.

5:6–8: Jn 19:34; 4:23; 15:26. **5:9:** Jn 5:32, 36; 8:18. **5:10:** 1 Jn 1:10.

---

stressed in 1 John (3:23; 5:10, 13), as well as in the Gospel of John (Jn 1:12; 3:16–18; 5:24, etc.). See note on Jn 3:36.

5:6 by water and blood: Alludes to the historical ministry of Jesus, which began with a baptism of water in the Jordan (Lk 3:21) and ended with a baptism of blood in Jerusalem (Lk 12:50). Again, John is emphasizing the full reality of Christ's humanity (CCC 463).

5:7-8 A handful of late Greek manuscripts, along with a few medieval Vulgate manuscripts and the Clementine Vulgate of 1592, expand these verses with the line: "There are three who give witness in heaven: the Father, the Word, and Holy Spirit, and these three are one" (inserted either in 5:7 or in 5:8 with minimal variation). This is known as the "Johannine Comma" or the "heavenly witnesses" text. Despite the fact that this line is a clear expression of trinitarian doctrine, the Holy Office decreed in 1927 that Catholic scholarship, after careful examination of the manuscript evidence, is not bound to accept the text as part of the original wording of 1 John. The reading does not appear in the *Nova Vulgata*, the updated edition of the Latin Vulgate Bible approved by Pope John Paul II (1979).

5:8 three witnesses: Evidence of Christ's humanity is present in the liturgy, where the **Spirit** never ceases to bring Christ to the world through the **water** of Baptism and the **blood** of the Eucharist. Faith in the Incarnation is thus supported by the joint testimony of history and liturgy. John was uniquely qualified to insist on this: he not only engaged in sacramental ministry, but he was the sole apostle to witness the Spirit, the water, and the blood come forth from the crucified body of Jesus (Jn 19:30, 34) (CCC 1108, 1225). See note on Jn 19:34. ● The Mosaic Law requires joint testimony from two or three witnesses to uphold a claim in court (Deut 19:15). For other uses of this legal standard in the NT, see Jn 5:30–47 and 2 Cor 13:1. ● The three witnesses become one in Baptism, for if you eliminate one of them, the sacrament ceases to be. Without the Cross of Christ, water is simply a natural element. Without water, there is no mystery of regeneration. And unless one is baptized in the name of the Father, the Son, and the Holy Spirit, there is neither remission of sins nor reception of spiritual grace (St. Ambrose, *On the Mysteries* 4, 20).

5:13 you have eternal life: John is certain, not that his readers will make it to heaven, but that they are filled with the living presence of Christ. This is how John understands "eternal life" throughout the letter (1:2; 3:14–15; 5:1–12, 20). Readers are thus assured that they *possess* Christ, not that they will *persevere* in his grace until the end. The danger still exists that the saints on earth can fall into deadly sin (5:16).

5:14 if we ask anything: The children of God (3:1) can approach the Father with the filial confidence that he hears us and desires to meet our needs (Lk 11:9–13). This is made possible through Christ, whose holy name gives us access to the heavenly throne (Jn 14:13–14; Heb 4:16; CCC 432).

5:16–17 John distinguishes between sin that is **deadly** (Gk., "unto death") and sin that is **not deadly** (Gk., "not unto death"). The reference is to spiritual death rather than physical death. Sinning unto death means sinning so grievously that one forfeits the indwelling "life" of Christ (5:12) and lapses back into a state of "death" (the reverse of 3:14). The evil in view is probably "apostasy", i.e., the sin of the heretical secessionists who denied the truth of apostolic doctrine (2:22) and severed themselves from the life and liturgy of the apostolic Church (2:19). Sin that does not lead to death weakens one's fellowship with God and requires cleansing and forgiveness (1:6–9) but does not extinguish the divine life abiding within (3:24). It is unclear why John does not ask believers to pray for persons guilty of deadly sins. Whatever the reason, his words do not imply that such a one is beyond the reach of God's mercy or incapable of future repentance. ● Catholic moral theology adopts this distinction between mortal and nonmortal (venial) sins. Venial offenses can be forgiven by prayers of contrition and other means, but, ordinarily, mortal sins cannot be forgiven apart from the absolution and restorative grace of the Sacrament of Reconciliation (CCC 1854–64). See note on 1 Jn 1:9.

5:18-20 John concludes with a synopsis of several themes from the letter. Each verse in succession declares what believers "know" with the certitude of faith.

5:18 does not sin: On the meaning of this, see note on 1 Jn 3:6.

5:20 the true God: An assertion of Christ's divinity that balances John's persistent emphasis on Christ's humanity (1:1–2; 4:2; 5:6–8; CCC 464). These words could describe the Father, but they more likely refer to **his Son Jesus Christ** in the preceding sentence. **eternal life:** Also a reference to Christ, who is the embodiment of divine life (1:2).

5:21 idols: The confession that Christ is the "true God" (5:20) implies that every pagan deity is a false god unworthy of worship. Idolatry was everywhere present in Asia Minor, where John's readers probably lived (CCC 2112).

---

[1] Greek *he*.

STUDY QUESTIONS: 1 JOHN

Chapter 1

For understanding

1. **1:1–4.** To what does this prologue to John's letter give witness? On whose behalf is he speaking? How does John describe the Incarnation in terms applicable to the sacraments of the Church? What sacrament might serve as an example, and how?

2. **1:5.** What does it mean to "live in the light"? Who else in Judaism shared this black-and-white view of the world?

3. **1:9.** What kind of confession of sin does John envision? In biblical terms, what does "confession" mean? To what should private confession of sins to God ordinarily lead us? How does Jesus imply this in John's Gospel? How do we know that confession of sin to a priest is not a peculiarity of the New Covenant?

For application

1. **1:1–4.** Has your reception of the sacraments, particularly Reconciliation and Eucharist, affected your personal relationship with Jesus Christ? In what way? What story (or, in John's word, "testimony") could you tell to illustrate the difference these sacraments make? How might such stories encourage others?

2. **1:5.** Refer to the note for this verse. How do you picture the world? To what extent would you share John's black-and-white view of it? If you are willing to tolerate "shades of gray" in yourself, how would your approach to sanctity compare with that of John—or, for that matter, with that of Jesus, who said, "He who is not with me is against me" (Mt 12:30), and, "He who loves father or mother more than me is not worthy of me" (Mt 10:37)?

3. **1:6–7.** *For private reflection*: Think about which of the Ten Commandments touches the area of greatest moral weakness for you. What are the issues you face in regard to that commandment or to the Church's teaching about it? Does your attitude or your behavior bring you closer to what John says in v. 6 or to what he says in v. 7?

4. **1:8–10.** How hard is it for you to prepare for the Sacrament of Reconciliation? How might these words of 1 John encourage us to take advantage of this cleansing sacrament more often?

Chapter 2

For understanding

1. **Word Study: Expiation (2:2).** What can the Greek term mean in reference to God? Or to sin? Which of these two meanings is meant in 1 John? What is the basis for this understanding in the OT Greek? In light of this OT background, how does John interpret the death of Jesus?

2. **2:15–17.** Why does John urge readers to let go of the world, since God both made it and loves it? What is man's natural inclination in regard to the world? Why do Jewish and Christian traditions promote the ascetical disciplines of prayer, fasting, and almsgiving?

3. **2:18.** If the "last hour" applies to the final phase of salvation history, what is this final phase? Also, what does the expression "antichrist" mean? How is its meaning sometimes restricted?

4. **2:20.** What does it mean to say that believers are "anointed"? What is the relationship between confessing Jesus as Messiah and receiving his anointing? What kind of anointing did Isaiah have in mind (Is 61:1)? What does Vatican II teach about this?

For application

1. **2:1–3.** How scrupulous is your conscience? For example, how do you feel about committing small infractions, such as blurting out an obscenity? What comfort can you derive from knowing that "Jesus Christ the righteous . . . is the expiation for our sins"?

2. **2:4–6.** How do you respond spiritually when you violate one of the Ten Commandments (taking into consideration, as well, the way the *Catechism* understands their application)? How seriously do you take such violations? What motivation can you derive from knowing that obeying the commandments helps bring the love of God to perfection?

3. **2:15–17.** Reflect on the note for these verses. How difficult would it be for you to give up your economic, social, or political status or have it taken away? If its removal would be hard for you, how might this attachment be affecting your love for God?

4. **2:26–27.** Consult the note for v. 20, especially the part about what Vatican II teaches. Although the "supernatural insight into the gospel (*sensus fidei*)" protects the Church *as a whole* from error, individual Christians can (and do) err about what the gospel says. What aspects of the gospel are unclear to you? What can you do to understand better Christ's teaching on these issues? How does the Church, enlightened by the Holy Spirit, provide guidance?

Chapter 3

For understanding

1. **3:1.** How do believers become children of God? To what does the grace of divine generation entitle us? If our standing as sons and daughters before God is not in name only, what is it?

2. **3:6.** What is John saying that true believers refuse to do? To what does John's focus on the moral life lead, and what point does he wish to make?

3. **3:16.** When it comes to laying down our lives, what two kinds of martyrdom does John have in mind? Who is called to which kind? How does John's plea to help the needy with tangible assistance fit into this?

4. **3:19–20.** How does a believer know that his heart is beating with the truth? How does the heart respond? What is a sure sign of alienation from the truth? What does John mean by saying that God is greater than our conscience?

For application

1. **3:1–3.** According to these verses, on what should a desire for personal holiness be based? How does the basis of your own desire for holiness compare with John's?

2. **3:4.** How does John define *sin*? Does John's definition include both moral and civil law?

3. **3:9.** Meditate on this verse. What does it mean to say that, if "God's seed abides" in you, you *cannot* sin? How might this consideration encourage you to avoid sin in the future?

4. **3:11–18.** According to John, loving your neighbor is essential for loving God. Do you ever get into a quarrel, especially one of a long-running nature? What have you done to resolve disagreements, grudges, or hurt feelings? If you cannot resolve them for some reason, how can you love those who have hurt you or whom you have hurt?

Chapter 4

For understanding

1. **4:1** What must John's readers distinguish? What practical test does John propose? Who are the false prophets about whom John is writing?

2. **4:8.** What does it mean to say that "God is love"? How does this divine love enter into history? How does John say that we can be sure God lives in us?

3. **Word Study: Confidence (4:17).** What else can the Greek word for "confidence" mean? How is it used with reference to speech? How does 1 John use the term?

4. **4:18.** How does love cast out fear? Over time, what does the exercise of charity instill?

For application

1. **4:1.** Consult the note for this verse. How would you test your own spiritual impulses, "senses", or urgings? Against what standard? Have you ever concluded that a spiritual impulse, "sense", or urge was not of the Holy Spirit? What brought you to that conclusion? What did you learn about discernment from it?

2. **4:4.** Compare this verse with 3:19-20. How might the recognition of the Holy Spirit's presence in you help allay any anxieties you may have about the world or its influence on you? According to 3:21-24 and 4:13-16, how do you know that the Holy Spirit really is in you? Compare John's criteria for recognizing the presence of the Spirit with those given in Gal 5:16-26.

3. **4:7-12.** According to v. 10 (and v. 19), where does our love for God and neighbor originate? What is the model of our love for one another? How is the love about which John is talking different from either liking or being attracted to someone?

4. **4:17-18.** How often do you think of the Day of Judgment, and what is your attitude toward it? When it comes to judgment, of what are you most afraid and why? Of what are you least afraid and why? How does love eliminate fear?

Chapter 5

For understanding

1. **5:6.** To what aspects of Jesus' historical ministry does John's expression "by water and blood" refer? What is John emphasizing?

2. **5:8.** How is evidence for the humanity of Christ shown to be continually present in the liturgy? That is, to what sacrament do the Spirit, the water, and the blood refer? Considering the Torah, explain why John would cite *three* witnesses.

3. **5:13.** By saying that his readers "have eternal life", what is John saying about them? Of what are readers thus assured—and *not* assured?

4. **5:16-17.** What is the difference between sins that are mortal (deadly) and sins that are not mortal? To what mortal sin does 1 John most likely refer? What does Catholic moral theology teach about the way mortal and venial sins can be forgiven?

For application

1. **5:3-4.** In your experience, how does faith lighten the burden of God's commandments? By contrast, how might lack of faith make the commandments more burdensome? What does "the world" have to do with the difficulty of following the commandments?

2. **5:14-15.** If we are children of God, why does he sometimes deny the requests we make of him? What does it mean, in practice, to pray "according to his [God's] will"? Think of an actual situation when you prayed for a particular outcome and felt your request was not granted—how might you have changed the nature of your prayer to be more closely conformed to God's will?

3. **5:16-17.** These verses are in the context of vv. 13-15. For what is John recommending that you pray—and why is that prayer according to the will of God? Consult the note for these verses: Why do you think John would not say that you should pray about mortal sin? If prayer alone cannot help someone who has fallen into grave sin, what can?

4. **5:19-21.** How can understanding the truth help you remain faithful to your Christian call in a world like ours? Granted that we no longer worship the idols familiar to John's readers, what might be the idols in your own life? How might you avoid them?

INTRODUCTION TO
THE SECOND LETTER OF SAINT JOHN

Author and Date The writer refers to himself, not by name, but by his title: "the elder" (2 Jn 1). Because the author of 3 John describes himself in the same way, and because the Johannine letters are doctrinally and stylistically quite similar to each other, Christian tradition has generally attributed all three of these epistles to a single author, namely, the Apostle John, son of Zebedee, one of the Twelve (Mk 3:17). Nevertheless, some scholars dispute both the apostolic and common authorship of 1, 2, and 3 John. Even in the ancient Church, an opinion circulated that 2 and 3 John did not come from the pen of the apostle. The basis for this judgment was a primitive tradition, traceable to the second-century bishop Papias of Hierapolis, that someone named "John the Elder" lived at the same time as John the Apostle and apparently in the same region of Ephesus in Asia Minor (quoted in Eusebius, *Ecclesiastical History* 3, 39). Though plausible, given the author's self-description in the opening verse, the evidence for attributing 2 John to this otherwise unknown figure is too slight to overturn the traditional ascription. On the other hand, the long-held conviction that all three letters come from the Apostle John is supported, not only by the strength of the evidence for John's authorship of 1 John, a view that was never seriously challenged in early Christian times, but also by an extensive list of similarities among the Johannine letters, especially between 1 and 2 John (e.g., compare 2 Jn 5 with 1 Jn 2:7; 2 Jn 7 with 1 Jn 2:18–22 and 4:1–2; and 2 Jn 12 with 1 Jn 1:4). These and other parallels suggest that 2 John not only comes from the same author as 1 John but was probably written about the same time, perhaps around A.D. 100. See introduction to 1 John: *Author* and *Date*.

Destination and Purpose The letter is written to a young missionary church under John's pastoral care. The location of this community is not specified, but presuming the reliability of the tradition that John spent his later years in Ephesus (see Irenaeus, *Against Heresies* 3, 1, 1), it is safe to conclude that the community was somewhere within the range of John's influence and authority in Asia Minor (southwestern Turkey). The letter warns believers of an approaching band of deceivers whose doctrines openly contradict apostolic tradition. Their denial that God became man in Jesus Christ is the most serious and disturbing of all (2 Jn 7). Readers are to stand guard against these incoming propagandists, who will likely attempt to spread confusion by infiltrating the house church where the community gathers for worship and instruction (10–11). John hopes the epistle will arrive in time to prevent just such a disaster.

Themes and Characteristics The Second Letter of John is one of the shorter writings in the NT. It is a brief pastoral letter from a shepherd to an endangered community of sheep. Though space did not allow for the development of theological or spiritual themes, John has managed to blend the right amount of commendation and caution to make a powerful impact on his readers. *Commendation* is in order for this church, called the "elect lady" (1), because the apostle is encouraged by their commitment to the truth and their persistent efforts to live out Jesus' commandment of love (4). John appeals to them to continue on the same course (5–6). *Caution* also is in order because false prophets are marching around Asia Minor with the erroneous idea that Jesus Christ never actually came "in the flesh" (7). These deceivers, under the guise of traveling missionaries, are bound to reach this area and attempt to worm their way into the community. Readers are forbidden to host them or even to greet them (10–11). The brief counsel delivered in this letter is only a prelude to the in-depth instruction that John hopes to give them in person (12). «

OUTLINE OF THE SECOND LETTER OF SAINT JOHN

1. **Opening Address (1–3)**

2. **Body of the Letter (4–12)**
   A. Loving One Another (4–6)
   B. Warning against Deceivers (7–11)
   C. Hope for a Future Visit (12)

3. **Closing Greeting (13)**

THE SECOND LETTER OF
SAINT JOHN

Salutation

1 The elder to the elect lady and her children, whom I love in the truth, and not only I but also all who know the truth, [2]because of the truth which abides in us and will be with us for ever:

3 Grace, mercy, and peace will be with us, from God the Father and from Jesus Christ the Father's Son, in truth and love.

Truth and Love

4 I rejoiced greatly to find some of your children following the truth, just as we have been commanded by the Father. [5]And now I beg you, lady, not as though I were writing you a new commandment, but the one we have had from the beginning, that we love one another. [6]And this is love, that we follow his commandments; this is the commandment, as you have heard from the beginning, that you follow love. [7]For many deceivers have gone out into the world, men who will not acknowledge the coming of Jesus Christ in the flesh; such a one is the deceiver and the antichrist. [8]Look to yourselves, that you may not lose what you [a] have worked for, but may win a full reward. [9]Any one who goes ahead and does not abide in the doctrine of Christ does not have God; he who abides in the doctrine has both the Father and the Son. [10]If any one comes to you and does not bring this doctrine, do not receive him into the house or give him any greeting; [11]for he who greets him shares his wicked work.

Final Greetings

12 Though I have much to write to you, I would rather not use paper and ink, but I hope to come to see you and talk with you face to face, so that our joy may be complete.

13 The children of your elect sister greet you.

1: 3 Jn 1.   **5:** Jn 13:34.   **6:** 1 Jn 5:3.   **7:** 1 Jn 2:22.   **12:** 1 Jn 1:4; 3 Jn 13.

---

1 The elder: Or, "the presbyter". The Greek term can refer to an elderly man or to an ordained shepherd of the Church, such as an apostle (1 Pet 5:1) or priest (Acts 14:23). John was both an apostle and an older man at the time of writing. See word study: *Elders* at Jas 5:14. **the elect lady:** Some think the addressee is an individual matron, named Electa or Kyria (the Greek is *eklektē kyria*). More likely, it is a local Church, as suggested by the greeting from a sister community in verse 13. John envisions this local congregation in the same way that Paul envisions the universal Church: as feminine and maternal (Eph 5:23; CCC 2040). See introduction to 2 John: *Themes and Characteristics*.

3 Grace, mercy, and peace: The same greeting is used in 1 and 2 Timothy and represents an expansion of the more usual formula, "grace and peace" (Rom 1:7; 1 Pet 1:2; Rev 1:4).

4 some of your children: The implication of this statement is uncertain. Either John had made contact with only "some" of his readers, and these he found obeying the gospel, or else he implies that only "some" of those he encountered were doing well, while others were not. The absence of any rebuke in the letter, along with the general affirmation in verse 8, seems to favor the former interpretation.

5 from the beginning: John's teaching about love is not new but is traceable back to the initial catechesis of his readers (6; 1 Jn 3:11). **love one another:** The supreme mandate that Christ has laid upon his disciples (Jn 13:34). The meaning of his words is explained by his example, which shows us that Christian love is not an emotion, but an act of the will that adheres to the commandments of God (Jn 14:31) and expresses itself through heroic generosity and sacrifice, even to the point of death (Jn 15:13).

7 many deceivers: Heretical teachers who denied that God the Son came **in the flesh** as a man. In doing so, they exchanged the truth of the gospel for lies and became "false prophets" who streamed out "into the world" with their errors (1 Jn 4:1) (CCC 465). Behind this warning is John's concern that these troublemakers might destroy the faith of others, as well (1 Jn 2:26). See note on 1 Jn 4:2. **the antichrist:** A title given to anyone who denies the Father and the Son and attacks the messianic claims of Jesus (1 Jn 2:22; CCC 675). See note on 1 Jn 2:18.

8 what you have worked for: The attainment of salvation (Phil 2:12) as well as additional rewards bestowed for faithful service (1 Cor 3:14).

9 one who goes ahead: The Greek text envisions someone who "goes beyond" the limits of authentic Christian doctrine. No hint is given as to their motives, but such individuals are often described as "progressives" who not only embrace novel teachings, but who leave behind the truths of apostolic faith in the process. **does not have God:** Faith in God and fellowship with God go hand in hand. John is insistent on this point and warns that breaking away from the true faith means breaking away from the one true God.

10 into the house: A house church used for Christian assembly. Private homes were a common venue for fellowship, catechesis, and liturgy in apostolic times (Acts 2:46; 1 Cor 16:19). John wants to block deceivers (2 Jn 7) from gaining admittance to these gatherings and disseminating their errors. Hospitality could prove harmful in this extreme situation.

12 paper: Literally, "papyrus". The limited writing space on a single sheet of papyrus probably determined the length of the letter. **face to face:** John voices his preference for personal rather than written instruction. The same sentiment is expressed in 3 Jn 13–14 and by Paul in 1 Cor 11:34.

13 your elect sister: An unnamed sister Church (possibly Ephesus) in the region.

---

[a] Other ancient authorities read *we*.

STUDY QUESTIONS: 2 JOHN

For understanding
1. **v. 1.** To what can the Greek word "presbyter" refer? Which of these was John? Who is the "elect lady" being addressed in this verse? How does John envision this local congregation?
2. **v. 5.** How far back can John's teaching about love be traced? How are the words of Christ's supreme mandate explained, and what does it show about love?
3. **v. 9.** To what does the expression "one who goes ahead" refer? What does John mean by saying that someone "does not have God"? With what is his warning concerned?
4. **v. 10.** In apostolic times, for what were private homes used? How could hospitality in this kind of environment become harmful?

For application
1. **v. 2.** What—or rather, who—is the "truth which abides in us"? What practical difference does it make to regard the truth as a person (particularly, a Person of the Trinity) instead of as a thing?
2. **v. 6.** How can following the commandments be a service of love to the Christian community? By contrast, how can failure or refusal to follow the commandments be a disservice to the community?
3. **v. 8.** How can you protect yourself from being deceived by false, misleading, trendy, or deceptive theological opinions? What efforts are you making to learn your faith at a level appropriate to your age?
4. **vv. 10–11.** Consult the note for v. 10. What do you think it means to "greet" a presenter of false teaching? How might extending an invitation to a dissenting theologian (for example, someone who advocates abortion) to speak in your parish involve you in his dissent?

INTRODUCTION TO
THE THIRD LETTER OF SAINT JOHN

Author The Third Letter of John is nearly identical in style, structure, and length to 2 John, and both have close affinities with 1 John. Interrelations of this type among the Johannine epistles support the common authorship of all three letters, which tradition generally attributes to John the Apostle, son of Zebedee and one of the Twelve (Mk 3:17). Indeed, it would be hard to account for the inclusion of such a short and incidental letter as 3 John in the canon of Scripture unless the epistle had a strong claim to apostolic authenticity in the ancient Church. Even on internal grounds, the Apostle John emerges as the most likely of any proposed candidate for authorship.

Date The same factors that suggest a single author wrote 1, 2, and 3 John also suggest the letters were written about the same time, probably around A.D. 100. A number of scholars contend that 3 John was actually the first of the three Johannine letters to be written, but this has not been determined with certainty. See introduction to 2 John: *Author and Date.*

Purpose Third John was written for several reasons: **(1)** to encourage the addressee, "Gaius" (1), in his efforts to show hospitality toward traveling preachers in need of temporary food and lodging (5–8); **(2)** to expose a certain "Diotrephes", whose heavy-handed leadership over a local Church was not to be endorsed or imitated (9–11); and **(3)** to recommend to Gaius a faithful brother named "Demetrius", who probably delivered this letter by hand (12).

Themes and Characteristics Third John holds the distinction of being the shortest writing in the NT. Its tone is generally warm and pastoral, and its contents are straightforward and practical. What is most distinctive about 3 John is the problem it addresses: jurisdictional rivalry among leaders in the primitive Church.

On the one side stands John, the apostle and shepherd over several Church communities, which tradition locates in Asia Minor. On the other side is Diotrephes, a leader in one of these local Churches, who is behaving more like a dictator than a pastor. When delegates or missionaries arrive from John, Diotrephes shuts them out. When opinions are voiced about John, he slanders the apostle with damaging words. When parishioners express their loyalty to John by hosting his emissaries, he drives them out of his community (9–10). John deals with this distressing situation by asking Gaius, already reputed for his hospitality (5–6), to keep both his heart and his home open to authentic preachers of the gospel (8, 12). Hope is held out that John might soon make an appearance to visit Gaius face to face (14) and to call Diotrephes to account for his tyrannical ways (10). «

OUTLINE OF THE THIRD LETTER OF SAINT JOHN

1. **Opening Address (1–4)**

2. **Body of the Letter (5–12)**
   A. Gaius Encouraged (5–8)
   B. Diotrephes Exposed (9–11)
   C. Demetrius Commended (12)

3. **Closing Greeting (13–15)**

THE THIRD LETTER OF
SAINT JOHN

Salutation

1 The elder to the beloved Ga´ius, whom I love in the truth.

Gaius Commended for His Service

2 Beloved, I pray that all may go well with you and that you may be in health; I know that it is well with your soul. [3]For I greatly rejoiced when some of the brethren arrived and testified to the truth of your life, as indeed you do follow the truth. [4]No greater joy can I have than this, to hear that my children follow the truth.

5 Beloved, it is a loyal thing you do when you render any service to the brethren, especially to strangers, [6]who have testified to your love before the Church. You will do well to send them on their journey as befits God's service. [7]For they have set out for his sake and have accepted nothing from the heathen. [8]So we ought to support such men, that we may be fellow workers in the truth.

Diotrephes and Demetrius

9 I have written something to the Church; but Diot´rephes, who likes to put himself first, does not acknowledge my authority. [10]So if I come, I will bring up what he is doing, accusing me falsely with evil words. And not content with that, he refuses himself to welcome the brethren, and also stops those who want to welcome them and puts them out of the Church.

11 Beloved, do not imitate evil but imitate good. He who does good is of God; he who does evil has not seen God. [12]Deme´trius has testimony from every one, and from the truth itself; I testify to him too, and you know my testimony is true.

Final Greetings

13 I had much to write to you, but I would rather not write with pen and ink; [14]I hope to see you soon, and we will talk together face to face.

15 Peace be to you. The friends greet you. Greet the friends, every one of them.

1: Acts 19:29; 2 Jn 1. **12:** Jn 21:24. **13:** 2 Jn 12.

---

1 The elder: The same pastoral title is used by the author of 2 John. Early Christian tradition generally identifies him as the Apostle John. **beloved:** An endearing tone runs through the letter, suggesting that John and his addressee have developed a deep, spiritual friendship (2, 5, 11). **Gaius:** Several persons of this name appear elsewhere in the NT, one from Macedonia (Acts 19:29), one from Derbe (Acts 20:4), and one from Corinth (1 Cor 1:14). The individual addressed in 3 John could be one of these men, but evidence is lacking to establish such a link with certitude. Nothing certain is known of this Gaius beyond his glowing reputation for holiness (3 Jn 3) and hospitality (5–6). Perhaps he was a recognized Church leader or simply a wealthy believer who gave food and lodging to preachers passing through the area.

2 be in health: Hellenistic letters commonly opened with a wish for good health. Gaius' spiritual health is something of which John is already confident (3).

4 my children: John speaks as a spiritual father who rejoices over the good behavior of his sons and daughters (1 Jn 2:1; 2 Jn 4).

7 for his sake: Literally, "for the name". Traveling preachers invite others to believe in the name of Jesus Christ (Jn 1:12). See note on 1 Jn 3:23. **from the heathen:** Pagans are not solicited to support the Church's ministers and missionaries, who are entitled to support from the community of believers. See note on Lk 10:7.

8 support such men: Gaius is urged to continue welcoming traveling teachers of the faith and equipping them with the basic necessities of life (6). In this way, he will help to facilitate the spread of gospel truth throughout the region.

9–10 A disturbing character sketch of Diotrephes. He is *insubordinate* to John's authority, he speaks *inappropriate* words against John, he is *inhospitable* to traveling preachers, and he is *intolerant* of any member of his congregation who welcomes them. Such audacious misuse of authority is merely a symptom of Diotrephes' pride and selfish quest to be "first" (9).

9 I have written: Some think this refers to 2 John. Others envision a letter of correction that John had addressed to the Church where Diotrephes held authority. It is no surprise that such a letter would not have survived, for the authority of its sender was rejected by the primary recipient.

11 not seen God: The notion of "seeing" has a theological rather than literal meaning. That is, one who has come to trust and obey Christ has come to "see" the Father and his love in the Son (Jn 14:9). Conversely, the one who remains in sin lacks this perception of God (1 Jn 3:6).

12 I testify to him: Demetrius appears to be the bearer of 3 John. If so, the letter also serves as a letter of recommendation for him. Many such letters were written in the ancient Church to prepare the way for traveling missionaries going from place to place (Acts 18:27; Rom 16:1–2; 2 Cor 3:1). John hopes Gaius will welcome godly men like Demetrius (3 Jn 8), whom Diotrephes turns away (10).

13 pen and ink: John has additional instruction for Gaius, but he prefers to communicate it in person rather than in writing (14; cf. 1 Cor 11:34; 2 Jn 12).

15 The friends: The members of John's Church, probably in Ephesus, and also the members of Gaius' Church, to whom their greetings are sent.

STUDY QUESTIONS: 3 JOHN

For understanding
1. **v. 1.** What was the relationship between John and Gaius? What do we know about Gaius?
2. **v. 7.** How were missionaries to be supported?
3. **vv. 9–10.** What do we learn about the character of Diotrephes from John's sketch of him? Of what is his misuse of authority a symptom?

For application
1. **v. 4.** If you have children or others for whose education you are responsible, what efforts have you made to ensure that they follow the truth (that is, live active Christian lives)? How do you feel when you see that your efforts are succeeding?
2. **v. 5.** What opportunities exist within your own parish community for practicing hospitality to strangers? Have you taken advantage of those opportunities?
3. **vv. 7–8.** What is your relationship with Catholic missions or missionaries? In what ways do you support them, both financially and spiritually? If you do not provide at least some financial support for missionary outreaches, what keeps you from doing so?
4. **v. 12.** What kinds of evangelization (those specifically aimed at spreading the truth of the gospel, not simply social action) does your parish support or engage in? How can you evangelize in your daily life?

INTRODUCTION TO
THE REVELATION TO SAINT JOHN

Author Four times the author of Revelation calls himself "John" (1:1, 4, 9; 22:8). He claims to be living in exile on the island of Patmos (1:9), where he received heavenly visions along with instructions to record them in a book (1:11, 19; 2:1, etc.). Christian tradition generally identifies him as the Apostle John, son of Zebedee (Mk 3:17) and the reputed author of the Gospel and epistles of John. Testimony supporting the apostolic authorship of Revelation comes from an array of ancient writers, including St. Justin Martyr (A.D. 165), St. Irenaeus (A.D. 180), St. Clement of Alexandria (A.D. 200), St. Hippolytus (A.D. 225), and St. Athanasius (ca. A.D. 350).

It must be noted, however, that this majority report is not the only report to have come down to us from Christian antiquity. Skepticism about whether the Apostle John authored the Book of Revelation surfaced in the middle of the third century, when Dionysius of Alexandria argued that the Greek idiom of Revelation differs so markedly from the other writings of John that it could not have been penned by the same author. He also noted that several key concepts in John's writings are absent from Revelation (e.g., life, truth, grace, joy) and that this absence weighs against a common authorship of Revelation and the other NT books attributed to the apostle (for the arguments of Dionysius, see Eusebius, *Ecclesiastical History* 7, 25). Most modern scholars agree with this assessment and therefore discount the tradition that connects Revelation to John the Apostle. Alternative theories of authorship have thus been formulated, though no consensus has been reached. The John of Revelation has been identified as **(1)** John the Baptist, **(2)** John Mark, the author of the Second Gospel, **(3)** an unknown prophet from Palestine named John, **(4)** John the Presbyter, a figure that some ancient writers contend was a contemporary of the Apostle John in Ephesus, and **(5)** an unidentified writer who used the apostle's name as a pseudonym in order to lend authority to his work. In the main, critical scholarship is content to think of the author of Revelation as a Christian prophet about whom nothing else is known.

Unfortunately, these alternative proposals require varying degrees of imagination and conjecture and are not without problems of their own. Hence there are still scholars who find the tradition of apostolic authorship historically credible and who argue that reasonable explanations can be given for the differences between Revelation and the other Johannine writings. Among the features of the book that fit well with the thesis of apostolic authorship, consider the following. **(1)** The mere mention of the name "John" without further specification suggests that the author was well known and had no need to assert his credentials or authority (1:1). It is assumed that readers would know who he was and would accept his words of instruction and correction without question. Conversely, if someone had simply been using the name John as a pseudonym, he would most likely have attached a title such as "apostle", lest it be unclear to readers whose authority was being invoked under that name. **(2)** The seven churches from Asia Minor addressed in Rev 2–3 are all within the region of Ephesus in Asia Minor where tradition says the Apostle John ministered in the later years of his life. **(3)** It is undeniable that the Book of Revelation reads quite differently from the Gospel and epistles of John. In itself, this does not rule out the possibility that a single author is responsible for all the books in question; after all, one should not expect works written in different literary genres to be very similar. But discrepancies in writing style and theological concepts are not so easily explained. This problem is especially acute for those scholars who assume all the writings traditionally ascribed to John to have been composed near the end of the first century. However, if Revelation appeared in the late 60s (as argued below), then as many as 30 years could stand between it and the publication of the Gospel and epistles in the late 90s. This could well explain why Revelation is written in a rough and heavily Semitic Greek, whereas the Gospel and epistles are written in smoother and more accurate Greek, yet still with a noticeable Semitic flavor. Such stylistic improvement is precisely the scenario one would expect from a Semitic speaker who learned Greek as a second language and whose command of its native idioms increased over the course of many years. As for theological concepts, it is true, as pointed out by Dionysius, that several key themes in the Fourth Gospel are not found in Revelation. Even so, this is not proof against their common authorship, for it is uncertain how much freedom the author of Revelation had in shaping the account of his visions. Presuming that he actually saw what he wrote down and that the prophetic and apocalyptic scenes he describes are not reducible to a literary device, we have little reason to think that the visionary had enough creative license to allow him to showcase his favorite theological concepts. Given this situation, it is remarkable that Revelation *does* share a number of common elements with the other Johannine writings, particularly the Gospel of John, that have no parallel in other NT writings. These include calling Jesus "the Word" (19:13; Jn 1:1, 14); describing the spiritual blessings of Jesus as "living water" (Rev 7:17; Jn 7:38); referring to Mary, the Mother of Jesus, as "woman" (Rev 12:1; Jn 19:26); and appealing to Zech 12:10 in reference to Jesus as the "pierced" Messiah (Rev 1:7; Jn 19:37).

None of the above considerations is sufficient by itself to support the apostolic authorship of Revelation. It is, rather, their cumulative force that is significant. Though one alleged author or another might seem plausible on the basis of a portion of the evidence, the apostle himself appears to correspond with all the evidence better than any other. Couple this with the widespread testimony of the early Church, and we continue to have solid reasons for attributing Revelation to the Apostle John.

Date No background information is more critical to the interpretation of Revelation than the date when the book was written. After all, much of its meaning is determined by the historical events and circumstances that John purports to explain. For the most part, ancient and modern scholars are divided between two alternatives: a clear majority date the book in the mid 90s of the first century, and a significant minority date it in the late 60s. **(1)** The majority view dates Revelation near the end of the reign of Emperor Domitian (A.D. 81 to 96). Support for this date is attested by ancient writers, including St. Irenaeus (A.D. 180), Victorinus of Pettau (A.D. 270), and St. Jerome (A.D. 370). Most modern scholars adopt this view, as well, and explain the symbolism of the book in terms of Christianity's life-and-death struggle with imperial Rome in the late first century. The demise of the harlot city in Rev 17–18 is often interpreted as God's judgment on pagan Rome. **(2)** The minority view dates Revelation near the end of the reign of Emperor Nero or shortly thereafter (A.D. 54 to 68). Ancient testimony to this date comes from the titles of Syriac versions of Revelation, which claim that John received these visions after being sent to the island of Patmos by Caesar Nero. Also, Andreas of Caesarea, a bishop in Cappadocia in the fifth century, says that several scholars in his day both dated and interpreted the Book of Revelation in connection with the Roman siege and destruction of Jerusalem in A.D. 70. Scholars who embrace this earlier date usually explain the theme of Christian suffering in terms of Jewish opposition to the gospel as well as the Neronian persecution that erupted in the mid 60s. They tend to see the fiery destruction of the harlot city in Rev 17–18 as the fall of Jerusalem. Despite the majority view, which puts

the composition of Revelation around A.D. 96, much of the internal evidence can be read to support a date before A.D. 70. All things considered, a date around A.D. 68 may be said to bring the greatest amount of clarity to the otherwise bewildering visions of the book.

Literary Background Revelation is the only book of its kind in the New Testament. On the one hand, it is a work of Christian prophecy that has much in common with the prophetic books of the Old Testament, especially Isaiah, Ezekiel, Daniel, and Zechariah. On the other, it is also an apocalyptic book with clear affinities to Jewish religious writings called apocalypses, which date from the same general time period (e.g., *1 Enoch, 4 Ezra, 2 Baruch, Apocalypse of Abraham*). These works display a comparable range of cosmic symbolism, heavenly visions, judgment scenes, and angelic mediators. Still, the Book of Revelation differs from its Jewish counterparts on several points. **(1)** Its author, John, writes in his own name (Rev 1:1) rather than using the name of a revered figure from the past, such as Enoch, Ezra, or Baruch. **(2)** Its focus on the triumph of Jesus Christ, the slain and risen Lamb, is unique when compared to other apocalyptic writings (5:6–8; 19:11–21). **(3)** It makes unprecedented use of liturgical hymns in revealing the worship that takes place in heaven (4:8, 11; 5:9–10, 13; 11:17–18; 15:3–4, etc.).

Being dominated by apocalyptic and prophetic symbolism, the Book of Revelation is notoriously difficult to interpret. Even St. Jerome, the most learned biblical scholar in the early Church, was compelled to admit that the Revelation of John "has as many mysteries as words" (*Letters* 53, 8). Its visions of hideous beasts and terrifying judgments seem part of a nightmare, while its scenes of worship, victory, and everlasting happiness seem part of a dream come true. These many sights and sounds are heavy with meaning, not least because John has worked a myriad of Old Testament allusions into the wording and structure of the book that constantly call readers back to the prophesies and types of biblical history. For these reasons, the book does not yield its secrets without effort. Only after prolonged study and contemplation of its mysteries in the light of Christian faith does one discover the powerful message of Revelation. Even then, many things remain obscure and invite us to further prayer and reflection about their intended meaning.

Interpretive Views Interpretations of Revelation usually follow one of five approaches that seek to explain the book by placing it within a particular frame of reference. **(1)** The *critical* view held by many scholars today situates the book within the cultural and historical context of its original readers. They tend to see in Revelation a reflection of the struggle between Church and State at the end of the first century. Its visions of judgment are often read as a Christian protest against the arrogance of secular Roman power and its pretensions to divine honor. So understood, the book proclaims that God will inevitably triumph over every human institution that opposes him and uses its authority for evil. **(2)** The *preterist* view likewise maintains that much of the book concerns events within the lifetime of its original readers. Scholars of this persuasion often assert that Revelation describes both the beginning of the New Covenant, sealed by the dying and rising of Christ, and the dramatic end of the Old Covenant, attested a generation later by the destruction of Jerusalem and the cessation of its Temple worship. The book is said to proclaim Christianity as the grand fulfillment of Old Testament hopes and the inauguration of salvation history's final and climactic phase. **(3)** The *historicist* view claims that Revelation offers a panorama of the Church's life as she marches through history. The successive visions of the book are said to correspond to successive stages of the Church's pilgrimage in the world, and its symbols are taken to represent important figures and institutions that determine the course of that history on a grand scale. In this view, the scope of the book can be said to encompass all of salvation history rather than to focus on a particular point in history. **(4)** The *idealist* view asserts that Revelation uses signs and symbols to dramatize the never-ending struggles of the spiritual life. Its visions of war between good and evil, angels and demons, etc., are said to represent the conflict that rages in every Christian's life. Though some would allow that Revelation refers to concrete events in the author's day, these are thought to typify the spiritual struggles between the Church and the world more generally. In this interpretation, Revelation offers a timeless message rather than a temporal message restricted to events of either the past or the future. **(5)** The *futurist* view, which seems to hold the greatest fascination in the popular mind, interprets the book as a preview of the end of history, the return of Christ, the Last Judgment, and the final demise of evil. Advocates thus claim that Revelation, either in whole or in part (e.g., chaps. 4–22), remains a book of prophecy for the Church today, for its many visions and promises still await their fulfillment in the days ahead.

In the final analysis, all these perspectives have something to offer and draw attention to important aspects of Revelation. What is needed is an *integrative* view that recognizes the presence of multiple themes and perspectives that complement one another and add richness and depth to the book. Christianity's struggle against the mighty Roman Empire is certainly part of the picture, as are the spiritual challenges to faith and fidelity that confront believers bombarded by the claims of the world. So too, one can hardly deny that Revelation offers a message of ultimate hope that looks ahead to the consummation of history and the heavenly glorification of the saints. Less commonly appreciated is the attention Revelation gives to the First Coming of Christ, whose death and Resurrection constitute the theological basis of the book, as well as the coming of Christ in judgment against unbelieving Jerusalem, which was known to the early Christians as the city "where their Lord was crucified" (11:8). «

OUTLINE OF THE REVELATION TO SAINT JOHN

1. **The Account of "What You See" (1:1–20)**
   A. Introduction (1:1–8)
   B. Inaugural Vision (1:9–20)

2. **The Account of "What Is" (2:1–3:22)**
   A. Letters to Ephesus, Smyrna, Pergamum, and Thyatira (2:1–29)
   B. Letters to Sardis, Philadelphia, and Laodicea (3:1–22)

3. **The Account of "What Is to Take Place" (4:1–22:21)**
   A. The Heavenly Liturgy of Creation and Redemption (4:1–5:14)
   B. The Seven Seals (6:1–8:5)
   C. The Seven Trumpets (8:6–11:19)
   D. The Seven Spiritual Figures (12:1–14:20)
   E. The Seven Bowls of Wrath (15:1–16:21)
   F. The Fall of the Harlot City (17:1–18:24)
   G. The Marriage Supper of the Lamb (19:1–10)
   H. The Judgment of the Beasts, the Devil, and the Dead (19:11–20:15)
   I. The New Heavens, New Earth, and New Jerusalem (21:1–22:5)

4. **Epilogue (22:6–21)**

THE REVELATION TO SAINT JOHN

Introduction and Salutation

1 The revelation of Jesus Christ, which God gave him to show to his servants what must soon take place; and he made it known by sending his angel to his servant John, ²who bore witness to the word of God and to the testimony of Jesus Christ, even to all that he saw. ³Blessed is he who reads aloud the words of the prophecy, and blessed are those who hear, and who keep what is written therein; for the time is near.

4 John to the seven churches that are in Asia:

Grace to you and peace from him who is and who was and who is to come, and from the seven spirits who are before his throne, ⁵and from Jesus Christ the faithful witness, the first-born of the dead, and the ruler of kings on earth.

To him who loves us and has freed us from our sins by his blood ⁶and made us a kingdom, priests to his God and Father, to him be glory and

---

1:4: Ex 3:14.   **1:5:** Ps 89:27.   **1:6:** Ex 19:6; Is 61:6.

1:1 gave him: In classic apocalyptic fashion, the revealed message comes from God through the mediation of heavenly beings, in this case through Jesus Christ and his angel (1:12–20; 22:16). **must soon take place:** A note of immediacy rings throughout the book, especially in the opening (1:3) and closing chapters (22:6–7, 10, 12, 20). The initial fulfillment of the book was thus expected within the lifetime of its first-century readers. • The expression alludes to the Greek version of Dan 2:28, where Nebuchadnezzar sees in a dream "what will be" in the latter days of the Messiah. The implication: what was still far off in Daniel's day is on the verge of fulfillment in John's day. **John:** Probably the Apostle John, a son of Zebedee (Mk 3:17). See introduction to Revelation: *Author.*
1:3 Blessed: The first of seven benedictions invoked upon those who heed the injunctions of the book (14:13; 16:15; 19:9; 20:6; 22:7, 14) (CCC 2626). **he who reads . . . those who hear:** The distinction between a single reader and mul-

tiple listeners implies a public reading of the book. Most likely this would take place in a liturgical setting, where the book would be read by a lector to a congregation assembled for worship. **prophecy:** As in the prophetic books of the OT, Revelation combines disclosures about the future with reflections on the past and appeals to remain faithful in the present.
1:4 the seven churches: Identified by name in 1:11 and addressed individually in chaps. 2–3. **Asia:** A Roman province in southwestern Turkey. **Grace . . . and peace:** A standard greeting in Christian correspondence (Rom 1:7; 1 Pet 1:2). By adding the farewell formula in Rev 22:21, John gives the entire book the character of a letter to be read in the liturgy (Col 4:16; 1 Thess 5:27). **him who is:** Implies that God is the eternal Lord of history. • The expression expands on the name of Yahweh revealed at the burning bush (Ex 3:14) (CCC 206, 212).
1:4–5 Grace and peace flow out from the Trinity, as seen in the threefold repetition of **from**, which is linked to the Father (**him who is**), the Son (**Christ**), and the Holy Spirit (**the seven spirits**). Christian interpreters have often read the "seven spirits" of Revelation as an allusion to the Spirit and his sevenfold gifts mentioned in Is 11:2 LXX (e.g., St. Ambrose, *On the Holy Spirit* 1, 16). Symbolic reflections of the Trinity also appear at Rev 5:6 and 22:1.
1:5 the first-born: The risen humanity of Jesus is the first specimen of God's new creation (21:5). • Jesus is described in the words of Ps 89:27, where Yahweh promises to exalt the messianic heir of David over every world ruler. This was fulfilled in Christ, who became "King of kings" (Rev 19:16) through his Resurrection and Ascension into heaven (Acts 2:29–36). See note on Rom 1:3. • Christ is called the first-born of the dead, not because he died before we did, but because he suffered death for us and was the first to rise again. Since he has risen, we too shall rise again through him (St. Athanasius, *Discourses against the Arians* 2, 61).
1:6 kingdom, priests: Believers share in the royal priesthood of Christ. This common priesthood of the faithful differs in kind and not simply in degree from the ministerial priesthood of the Church (CCC 1546). See note on 1 Pet 2:9. • Since the King of kings and Priest of heaven united us with his body when he offered himself for us, there is not one among the saints who does not possess the office of priesthood, for each is a member of the eternal Priest (St. Bede, *Explanation of the Apocalypse* 1, 6).

Word Study

Revelation (1:1)

Apokalypsis (Gk.): a noun meaning "revelation" or "unveiling". In the Bible, the term always refers to a disclosure of something that was previously unknown, whether it be secrets (Sir 22:22), works (Sir 11:27), the knowledge of God (Eph 1:17), or the plan of salvation (Eph 3:3). Mysteries can be made known in the present, such as Christ's glory and Lordship (Gal 1:12), or await disclosure until the future, when God will judge the world (Rom 2:5) and bestow glory on his children (Rom 8:19). The word *apokalypsis* serves as a title for the Book of Revelation, sometimes called the Apocalypse on the basis of this Greek term (Rev 1:1). The title is well chosen inasmuch as Revelation removes the veil from God's plan for the future, drawing back the curtain that hides Christ's glory, kingship, and control over history from the naked eye (Rev 4–5) (CCC 50).

---

dominion for ever and ever. Amen. [7]Behold, he is coming with the clouds, and every eye will see him, every one who pierced him; and all tribes of the earth will wail on account of him. Even so. Amen.

8 "I am the Alpha and the Omega," says the Lord God, who is and who was and who is to come, the Almighty.

A Vision of Christ

9 I John, your brother, who share with you in Jesus the tribulation and the kingdom and the patient endurance, was on the island called Patmos on account of the word of God and the testimony of Jesus. [10]I was in the Spirit on the Lord's day, and I heard behind me a loud voice like a trumpet [11]saying, "Write what you see in a book and send it to the seven churches, to Ephesus and to Smyrna and to Per´gamum and to Thyati´ra and to Sardis and to Philadelphia and to La-odice´a."

12 Then I turned to see the voice that was speaking to me, and on turning I saw seven golden lampstands, [13]and in the midst of the lampstands one like a Son of man, clothed with a long robe and with a golden sash across his chest; [14]his head and his hair were white as white wool, white as snow; his eyes were like a flame of fire, [15]his feet were like burnished bronze, refined as in a furnace, and his voice was like the sound of many waters; [16]in his right hand he held seven stars, from his mouth issued a sharp two-edged sword, and his face was like the sun shining in full strength.

17 When I saw him, I fell at his feet as though dead. But he laid his right hand upon me, saying, "Fear not, I am the first and the last, [18]and the living one; I died, and behold I am alive for evermore, and I have the keys of Death and Hades. [19]Now write what you see, what is and what is to take place hereafter. [20]As for the mystery of the seven stars which you saw in my right hand, and the seven golden lampstands, the seven stars are the angels of the seven churches and the seven lampstands are the seven churches.

The Message to Ephesus

2 "To the angel of the Church in Ephesus write: 'The words of him who holds the seven stars in his right hand, who walks among the seven golden lampstands.

1:7: Dan 7:13; Mt 24:30; Mk 14:62; Zech 12:10. **1:8:** Ex 3:14. **1:13:** Dan 7:13; 10:5.
1:15: Ezek 1:24. **1:16:** Ex 34:29. **1:17:** Is 44:2, 6.

1:7 he is coming: The towering expectation of the book, here described in the words of Dan 7:13 and Zech 12:10. • Daniel sees the Son of man riding the clouds into heaven, where the divine court grants him an everlasting kingdom that results in the destruction of his enemies. Zechariah portrays Israel mourning the death of its pierced and rejected Messiah. John blends these visions into one: Christ is the Son of man whose exaltation as king brings a sentence of judgment on those who pierced him. The passage may have provisional reference to the coming of Christ in judgment against unbelieving Jerusalem, the city that pierced him (Rev 11:8) and within a generation lay in ruins (Mt 22:7; 24:1–34). Ultimately, however, its fulfillment awaits the return of Christ in glory, when all peoples will behold his splendor and lament their participation in sin (Acts 1:11).

1:8 Alpha . . . Omega: The first and last letters of the Greek alphabet. They signify that God is the origin and destiny of all creation, as well as its sovereign Lord (22:13). • The same idea is expressed in a similar way in Is 41:4, 44:6, and 48:12.

1:9 Patmos: A small island in the southern Aegean Sea that was used by the Romans as a penal colony for criminals. John was banished there for being a Christian.

1:10 in the Spirit: John is seized by the Spirit while engaged in prayer and worship (see Jn 4:23–24). He is carried off into heaven (Rev 4:2), into the wilderness (17:3), and then to the summit of a high mountain (21:10). • Ezekiel was similarly transported to various locations by the Spirit (Ezek 2:2; 3:14; 11:1; 40:2). **the Lord's day:** Sunday, the first day of the week, when Christians gather for liturgy (Acts 20:7) to commemorate the Resurrection of Jesus (Lk 24:1–7) (CCC 1166–67).

1:12–17 The inaugural vision of Revelation. Borrowing images from Ezekiel and Daniel, it describes Jesus in both divine and human terms. • His hair is white like that of the Lord, the Ancient of Days (Dan 7:9), and his voice is like the rumbling of God's glory when it draws near (Ezek 43:2). His appearance also resembles a man (Dan 7:13) whose eyes are torches and whose feet gleam like bronze fired in a furnace

(Dan 10:6). John, like the prophets before him, falls prostrate before the exalted Lord (Rev 1:17; Ezek 1:28; 44:4; Dan 10:9).

1:12 seven golden lampstands: Each one is modeled on the branched candelabra, or *menorah*, that flickered in the sanctuaries of Israel (Ex 25:31–39). They symbolize the seven Churches addressed by John (Rev 1:20). • The passage evokes Zech 4:2, where a Temple menorah burns with the oil of the Spirit. This is a reminder that the seven Churches remain aglow with the Spirit and depend on him to enlighten others. • The Church's preaching is steady and true, and through it one and the same salvation radiates throughout the world. Announcing the truth everywhere, the Church is the seven-branched candlestick that bears the light of Christ (St. Irenaeus, *Against Heresies* 5, 20, 1).

1:13 long robe: A vestment worn by a high priest (Ex 28:4; Sir 45:8). Similar attire is worn by the heavenly angels (Rev 15:6). Jesus ministers to the needs of the seven Churches just as the Temple priests tended the *menorah* lamps by trimming their wicks and replenishing their oil (Ex 27:20–21) (CCC 662).

1:18 keys of Death and Hades: Symbolizes that Christ has royal and judicial power over life and death (3:7), which is the power to lock and unlock the gates of the underworld, called Hades (9:1; 20:1, 13; Wis 16:13–14) (CCC 633–35). See note on Mt 16:18.

1:19 what . . . what . . . what: A basic outline of the book. What John *sees* is chap. 1, *what is* refers to the present state of the Churches addressed in chaps. 2–3, and what is about to unfold *hereafter* is narrated in chaps. 4–22.

1:20 the angels: Perhaps a reference to the bishops or pastors of the seven churches, for each of the seven letters that follow is sent to an "angel" of the community (2:1, 8, 12, 18; 3:1, 7, 14).

2:1–3:22 John addresses seven churches in Asia Minor that lie within a 50-mile radius of one another. **(1)** Traditionally, it is held that the Apostle John settled in this area and ministered to these very churches in the later years of his life. **(2)** Geographically, the sequence of churches moves clockwise from Ephesus to Laodicea and may reflect the postal route of the day. **(3)** Structurally, each letter begins with an image that appeared

2 "'I know your works, your toil and your patient endurance, and how you cannot bear evil men but have tested those who call themselves apostles but are not, and found them to be false; [3]I know you are enduring patiently and bearing up for my name's sake, and you have not grown weary. [4]But I have this against you, that you have abandoned the love you had at first. [5]Remember then from what you have fallen, repent and do the works you did at first. If not, I will come to you and remove your lampstand from its place, unless you repent. [6]Yet this you have, you hate the works of the Nicola´-itans, which I also hate. [7]He who has an ear, let him hear what the Spirit says to the churches. To him who conquers I will grant to eat of the tree of life, which is in the paradise of God.'

The Message to Smyrna

8 "And to the angel of the Church in Smyrna write: 'The words of the first and the last, who died and came to life.

2:7: Gen 2:9.   2:8: Is 44:6.

---

in chap. 1 and ends with an allusion to chaps. 19–22. **(4)** Spiritually, the zeal of these churches is declining, with Ephesus in the best shape and Laodicea in the worst. **(5)** Historically, these letters allude to concrete circumstances and experiences of Asian Christians in the first century.

2:1 Ephesus: The most prestigious cultural, commercial, and religious center in the Roman province of Asia. Paul established the Church there (Acts 19:1–10) and later commissioned Timothy to build on his foundation (1 Tim 1:3). It is uncertain as to when John assumed pastoral responsibility over Ephesus and the other churches in the region.

2:4 abandoned the love: The Ephesians had turned their hearts away from Christ and let their enthusiasm for Christian living die down (Mt 24:12). According to Jesus, this constitutes a spiritual "fall" from which they must recover (Rev 2:5).

2:5 remove your lampstand: The price of impenitence is divine judgment. The threat of removal may recall the historical plight of Ephesus, a city that was twice forced to relocate because of the silting of its river and harbor.

2:6 the Nicolaitans: Early tradition links these heretics with Nicolaus, one of the seven deacons ordained in Acts 6:5. Whatever their background and origin, the Nicolaitans are said to have had a dangerously casual attitude toward idolatry and sexual immorality. Their corruptive influence was already at work among believers in Pergamum (Rev 2:15).

2:7 him who conquers: The one whose commitment to Jesus triumphs over every temptation to compromise or lose faith. The seven letters reveal the eternal rewards that await the saints who persevere (2:11, 17, 26; 3:5, 12, 21). **tree of life:** Signifies everlasting life and communion with Christ (22:14). Perhaps the promise is a strike at the Greek fertility goddess, Artemis, whose temple was located in Ephesus and who was sometimes depicted as a fruitful tree. ● Humanity was barred from the tree of life after the rebellion in Eden (Gen 3:22), but access has been regained through Christ, who gives a foretaste of its blessings in the Eucharist. See note on Jn 6:58.

2:8 Smyrna: Thirty miles north of Ephesus. Smyrna was fiercely loyal to Rome, a supporter of emperor worship, and

The Seven Churches of the Apocalypse

9 "'I know your tribulation and your poverty (but you are rich) and the slander of those who say that they are Jews and are not, but are a synagogue of Satan. [10]Do not fear what you are about to suffer. Behold, the devil is about to throw some of you into prison, that you may be tested, and for ten days you will have tribulation. Be faithful unto death, and I will give you the crown of life. [11]He who has an ear, let him hear what the Spirit says to the churches. He who conquers shall not be hurt by the second death.'

The Message to Pergamum

12 "And to the angel of the Church in Per´gamum write: 'The words of him who has the sharp two-edged sword.

13 "'I know where you dwell, where Satan's throne is; you hold fast my name and you did not deny my faith even in the days of An´tipas my witness, my faithful one, who was killed among you, where Satan dwells. [14]But I have a few things against you: you have some there who hold the teaching of Balaam, who taught Balak to put a stumbling block before the sons of Israel, that they might eat food sacrificed to idols and practice immorality. [15]So you also have some who hold the teaching of the Nicola´itans. [16]Repent then. If not, I will come to you soon and war against them with the sword of my mouth. [17]He who has an ear, let him hear what the Spirit says to the churches. To him who conquers I will give some of the hidden manna, and I will give him a white stone, with a new name written on the stone which no one knows except him who receives it.'

The Message to Thyatira

18 "And to the angel of the Church in Thyati´ra write: 'The words of the Son of God, who has eyes like a flame of fire, and whose feet are like burnished bronze.

19 "'I know your works, your love and faith and service and patient endurance, and that your latter works exceed the first. [20]But I have this against you, that you tolerate the woman Jez´ebel, who calls herself a prophetess and is teaching and beguiling my servants to practice immorality and to eat food sacrificed to idols. [21]I gave her time to repent, but she refuses to repent of her immorality. [22]Behold, I will throw her on a sickbed, and those who commit adultery with her I will throw into great tribulation, unless they repent of her doings; [23]and I will strike her children dead. And all the churches shall know that I am he who searches mind and heart, and I will give to each of you as

---

2:10: Dan 1:12.   **2:14:** Num 31:16; 25:1–2.   **2:17:** Ps 78:24; Is 62:2.   **2:18:** Dan 10:6.
2:20: 1 Kings 16:31; 2 Kings 9:22, 30; Num 25:1.   **2:23:** Jer 17:10; Ps 62:12.

---

home to a large Jewish community openly hostile to Christianity. Destroyed in 600 B.C. and refounded in 300 B.C., the city is addressed by him who truly **died** and **came to life** again.

2:9 synagogue of Satan: The perpetrators of Christian persecution in Smyrna are Jewish. Because Jews were the only ones in the Roman Empire legally exempt from worshiping the emperor and participation in the imperial cult, they could easily betray Christians to the Roman authorities for confessing Jesus as Lord (instead of Caesar) and practicing what was still an unauthorized religion in the eyes of Rome (Acts 14:2; 17:5–8). For Paul's estimate of what constitutes a true Jew, see Rom 2:17–29.

2:10 ten days: Possibly an allusion to the pagan rites of Niobe, practiced in Smyrna, whose devotees underwent ten days of mourning. • Daniel and his friends were also tested for ten days lest they compromise their faith by eating foods contaminated by idolatry (Dan 1:8–14). **the crown of life:** Means the crown that is (eternal) life. See note on Jas 1:12.

2:11 the second death: The eternal death of hell, described as a "lake of fire" (20:14; 21:8).

2:12 Pergamum: Forty-five miles northeast of Smyrna. Pergamum distinguished itself as the earliest and most enthusiastic center of emperor worship in the region. This and other forms of pagan religion made it the seat of "Satan's throne" (2:13).

2:13 Antipas: An early Christian martyr of whom nothing else is known.

2:14 teaching of Balaam: Certain troublemakers were permitting what the Jerusalem Council had prohibited: the consumption of idol food and the practice of sexual immorality (Acts 15:29). On the relation between this prohibition and Paul's teaching in 1 Cor 8–10, see essay: *Paul, Idol Food, and the Jerusalem Council* at 1 Cor 9. • Balaam appears in Num 22–24 as a Mesopotamian magician who counseled Moabite women to seduce the men of Israel into sexual and idolatrous sin (Num 25:1–3; 31:16). The warning that perpetrators of sin will face Christ's word of judgment, symbolized as a sword (Rev 2:16), recalls how Balaam was eventually slain with the sword (Num 31:8).

2:15 the Nicolaitans: See note on Rev 2:6.

2:17 the hidden manna: Refers to Christ himself, whose glory is concealed in heaven but whose coming in history (Incarnation) and liturgy (Eucharist) was foreshadowed in the gift of the manna given to Israel. See note on Jn 6:32. • Manna was the bread that Yahweh gave to the pilgrims of the Exodus, a sample of which was hidden away in the Ark of the Covenant (Ex 16:31–34; Heb 9:4). **a white stone:** Used in the ancient world to cast a vote of acquittal or carried as a pass to gain entrance into invitation-only assemblies. The believer is thus shown to be righteous or innocent, as well as invited to the marriage feast of the Lamb (19:7–9). **a new name:** A new identity in Christ (19:12) that admits believers into the heavenly presence of the Lord and the Lamb (22:3–4; Is 62:2) (CCC 2159).

2:18 Thyatira: Forty miles southeast of Pergamum. Thyatira was originally a military outpost that evolved into a commercial city famous for its trade guilds (Acts 16:14). These guilds had patron deities that its members were expected to honor in idolatrous ways. Failure to do so could mean both social disgrace and financial disaster for the conscientious Christian objector.

2:20 Jezebel: A false prophetess leading believers astray into religious idolatry and sexual impurity. These sins are direct violations of the pastoral decree issued by the Jerusalem Council (Acts 15:29). • The "Jezebel" of Revelation harkens back to Jezebel, the Sidonian wife of Ahab, king of Israel (1 Kings 16:31), and the chief adversary of the prophet Elijah (1 Kings 19:1–2). Jezebel ruthlessly slaughtered the innocent (1 Kings 21:1–16) and was infamous for her harlotries and sorcery (2 Kings 9:22).

2:23 as your works deserve: Christ will judge the churches for their deeds, rewarding the righteous with eternal life and repaying the wicked with everlasting death (20:12). The doctrine of judgment according to works is also taught by Paul (Rom 2:6–8) and the OT (Ps 62:12) (CCC 679).

your works deserve. [24]But to the rest of you in Thyati´ra, who do not hold this teaching, who have not learned what some call the deep things of Satan, to you I say, I do not lay upon you any other burden; [25]only hold fast what you have, until I come. [26]He who conquers and who keeps my works until the end, I will give him power over the nations, [27]and he shall rule them with a rod of iron, as when earthen pots are broken in pieces, even as I myself have received power from my Father; [28]and I will give him the morning star. [29]He who has an ear, let him hear what the Spirit says to the churches.'

The Message to Sardis

3 "And to the angel of the Church in Sardis write: 'The words of him who has the seven spirits of God and the seven stars.

" 'I know your works; you have the name of being alive, and you are dead. [2]Awake, and strengthen what remains and is on the point of death, for I have not found your works perfect in the sight of my God. [3]Remember then what you received and heard; keep that, and repent. If you will not awake, I will come like a thief, and you will not know at what hour I will come upon you. [4]Yet you have still a few names in Sardis, people who have not soiled their garments; and they shall walk with me in white, for they are worthy. [5]He who conquers shall be clothed like them in white garments, and I will not blot his name out of the book of life; I will confess his name before my Father and before his angels. [6]He who has an ear, let him hear what the Spirit says to the churches.'

The Message to Philadelphia

7 "And to the angel of the Church in Philadelphia write: 'The words of the holy one, the true one, who has the key of David, who opens and no one shall shut, who shuts and no one opens.

8 " 'I know your works. Behold, I have set before you an open door, which no one is able to shut; I know that you have but little power, and yet you have kept my word and have not denied my name. [9]Behold, I will make those of the synagogue of Satan who say that they are Jews and are not, but lie—behold, I will make them come and bow down before your feet, and learn that I have loved you. [10]Because you have kept my word of patient endurance, I will keep you from the hour of trial which is coming on the whole world, to try those who dwell upon the earth. [11]I am coming soon; hold fast what you have, so that no one may seize your crown. [12]He who conquers, I will make him a pillar in the

---

2:26: Ps 2:8–9.   **3:5:** Ex 32:32; Ps 69:28; Dan 12:1; Mt 10:32.   **3:7:** Is 22:22.
3:9: Is 60:14; 49:23; 43:4.   **3:12:** Is 62:2; Ezek 48:35; Rev 21:2.

2:24 the deep things of Satan: May suggest that the followers of Jezebel dabbled in sorcery and astrology, i.e., occult arts that lead practitioners to spiritual ruin (21:8).

2:27 rod of iron: Conquerors will possess in full what they already possess in part: a share in Christ's reign over the world (5:10; 22:5). • The iron rod calls to mind Ps 2:8–9, where David's royal heir is offered dominion over all nations. Solomon's empire, though the largest of any Davidic king in the OT, was only a faint approximation of the worldwide kingdom ruled by Christ (Mt 28:18–19; Rom 1:3–5). A rod or scepter figures in other messianic prophesies, as well (Gen 49:10; Num 24:17).

2:28 morning star: A name for the planet Venus, visible just before daybreak. It was a symbol of victory in pagan antiquity that later became a symbol of Christ's Resurrection and victory over death (22:16; 2 Pet 1:19). The promise here is a bodily resurrection and may also allude to the believer's triumph over the dark forces at work in pagan astrological practices.

3:1 Sardis: Thirty miles southeast of Thyatira. Sardis was once a wealthy and powerful city struggling to recover its former glory. Though a fortified city, it was twice conquered by surprise nighttime attacks. Christ may allude to this history when he warns readers to stay "awake" lest he come like a "thief" and the Church fare as badly as the unprepared city (3:3).

3:3 like a thief: This image can be traced back to Jesus (Mt 24:43; Lk 12:39).

3:4 soiled their garments: The white garments worn by angels and saints (4:4; 6:11; 7:9; 19:14) symbolize both purity and victory (Dan 11:35; 12:10) and were used in the ancient Church to clad the newly baptized. Some in Sardis had stained their robes by reverting to sinful ways and renewing their friendship with the world.

3:5 the book of life: A heavenly register of the saints. To be erased from this book is to lose the inheritance of eternal life (Ex 32:32; Ps 69:28). See note on Rev 20:12.

3:7 Philadelphia: Twenty-eight miles southeast of Sardis. Philadelphia served as a base for spreading Greek culture throughout the highlands of central Asia Minor. It was also home to a synagogue community hostile to Christians. **key of David:** A symbol of royal Davidic authority. Jesus holds this key as a descendant of David (Rom 1:3) and the messianic heir to his throne (Lk 1:32). • The expression comes from Is 22:22, where the keys of the house of David pass from one prime minister to another. Being the Davidic king, Christ possesses the fullness of royal power, yet the Church is given a share in his authority. See note on Mt 16:19.

3:8 an open door: Either missionary opportunities (1 Cor 16:9; Col 4:3) or access to the heavenly liturgy where God is perpetually worshiped (Rev 3:20; 4:1).

3:9 synagogue of Satan: Harassment from local Jews was a problem in Philadelphia as well as in Smyrna. See note on Rev 2:9. **before your feet:** The synagogue will be forced to acknowledge that the Church is the beloved people of the New Covenant (Is 60:14).

3:10 the hour of trial: A time of tribulation that will test the faith of believers. Jesus says it will seize the whole *oikoumenē*, a Greek term that often refers to the Mediterranean world ruled by Rome (cf. Lk 2:1; Acts 24:5). The warning may refer to the spiritual confusion, political chaos, and natural catastrophes that swept over the Roman world in the late 60s (Mt 24:4–13; Tacitus, *Histories* 1, 2). However, if one dates Revelation in the 90s, the best candidate is the persecution of Christianity under Emperor Domitian (A.D. 81 to 96). Believers in ancient Philadelphia are promised the Lord's protection from the widespread suffering. There is no hint that the text envisions a "rapture" of the Church into heaven before the onset of earthly distress.

3:12 pillar in the temple: Believers form a living temple indwelt with the Spirit and glory of God (Eph 2:19–22). To be a pillar is to stand in an honored position (Gal 2:9). The stability of a pillar contrasts with the instability of the city, which was leveled by an earthquake in A.D. 17. **my God:** Jesus is not denying his own divinity but speaks from the standpoint of his humanity, which he shares in common with us (as in Jn 20:17). **the name:** The righteous will bear the names of the Father and

temple of my God; never shall he go out of it, and I will write on him the name of my God, and the name of the city of my God, the new Jerusalem which comes down from my God out of heaven, and my own new name. [13]He who has an ear, let him hear what the Spirit says to the churches.'

The Message to La-odicea

14 "And to the angel of the Church in La-odice´a write: 'The words of the Amen, the faithful and true witness, the beginning of God's creation.

15 "'I know your works: you are neither cold nor hot. Would that you were cold or hot! [16]So, because you are lukewarm, and neither cold nor hot, I will spew you out of my mouth. [17]For you say, I am rich, I have prospered, and I need nothing; not knowing that you are wretched, pitiable, poor, blind, and naked. [18]Therefore I counsel you to buy from me gold refined by fire, that you may be rich, and white garments to clothe you and to keep the shame of your nakedness from being seen, and salve to anoint your eyes, that you may see. [19]Those

whom I love, I reprove and chasten; so be zealous and repent. [20]Behold, I stand at the door and knock; if any one hears my voice and opens the door, I will come in to him and eat with him, and he with me. [21]He who conquers, I will grant him to sit with me on my throne, as I myself conquered and sat down with my Father on his throne. [22]He who has an ear, let him hear what the Spirit says to the churches.'"

The Heavenly Worship

4 After this I looked, and behold, in heaven an open door! And the first voice, which I had heard speaking to me like a trumpet, said, "Come up here, and I will show you what must take place after this." [2]At once I was in the Spirit, and behold, a throne stood in heaven, with one seated on the throne! [3]And he who sat there appeared like jasper and carnelian, and round the throne was a rainbow that looked like an emerald. [4]Round the throne were twenty-four thrones, and seated on the thrones were twenty-four elders, clothed in white garments, with golden crowns upon their heads. [5]From the throne

---

3:14: Ps 89:28; Prov 8:22; Jn 1:1–3.   **3:17:** Hos 12:8.   **3:19:** Prov 3:12.   **4:1:** Ex 19:16, 24.
4:2: Ezek 1:26–28.   **4:5:** Ex 19:16; Zech 4:2.

---

the Son (14:1) and be identified as citizens of the heavenly Jerusalem (21:2-4). This may recall how Philadelphia was re-named (Neo-Caesarea) after the earthquake.

3:14 Laodicea: Forty miles southeast of Philadelphia. Laodicea was a prosperous commercial city that rebuilt itself without the aid of government subsidies after an earthquake around A.D. 60. It was known for its banking establishments, its medical academy, and its exported products, such as eye ointment and black wool textiles. According to Jesus, its material prosperity merely disguised its spiritual poverty (3:17). **the Amen:** A Hebrew acclamation used as a title for Christ. Expressing a sense of reliability and trustworthiness, it indicates that Jesus embodies the covenant faithfulness of God, for through him all the promises of God are carried to fulfillment. See word study: *Amen* at 2 Cor 1:20. ● The title comes from Is 65:16, where the Hebrew text underlying "the God of truth" is literally "the God of Amen" (CCC 1063-65). **the beginning:** The Greek term is capable of several meanings, ranging from "starting point" to "first cause" to "ruler". Christ is the divine Alpha, or first cause, that brought all creation into being (22:13). Identical language is used of God the Father (21:6).

3:16 lukewarm: Unlike nearby Colossae, Laodicea had no cold drinking water, and unlike nearby Hierapolis, it had no hot medicinal springs. On a spiritual level, the Church had become so complacent that the Lord promises to spit them out like a mouthful of tepid water.

3:18 buy from me: Ironically, local industries cannot provide what the Laodicean Church lacks most, since even a surplus of money, black wool, and eye salve cannot compare to the spiritual wealth, white garments, and supernatural sight supplied by Jesus. See note on Rev 3:14.

3:20 I stand at the door: Jesus is pictured standing outside the door of the Laodicean Church. ● An allusion is made to Song 5:2, where the bridegroom knocks lovingly on the door of his bride's chamber. Similar imagery appears in Rev 19:7-9.

3:21 sit with me: The conqueror is promised the fullness of a blessing he already enjoys in part, namely, a share in Christ's reign over the world (5:10; 20:4, 6; cf. Eph 2:6). Christ is already reigning with the Father in his risen humanity (11:15; 12:5; 22:1).

4:1—5:14 The third phase of the book (1:19) begins as the Spirit lifts John into heaven at the invitation of Christ. He is bombarded with a spectacular display of angels and saints

worshiping the Lord and the Lamb. The two chapters divide according to this dual focus of worship: Rev 4 praises the Father as the Maker of all (liturgy of creation), and Rev 5 praises the Son as the Savior of all (liturgy of redemption). ● The liturgical setting in heaven alludes to the cultic figures and fixtures of the Jerusalem Temple. Familiar sights and sounds include the throne (ark, 2 Sam 6:2), the seven torches (menorah, Ex 25:31-39), the winged creatures (cherubim, Ezek 1:10), the 24 elders (24 priestly divisions, 1 Chron 24:1-19), the glassy sea (molten sea, 1 Kings 7:23-26), the musical praise (psalms, 1 Chron 25:1-8), the golden bowls (dishes for incense, 1 Kings 7:50), and the sacrificial Lamb (Passover, Ex 12:21). This and similar scenes throughout the book (Rev 7:9-15; 8:1-5; 11:19; 15:2-8) express the ancient belief that the Temple of Jerusalem was a visible replica of the invisible sanctuary of God in heaven (Ex 26:30; Ps 11:4; Wis 9:8) (CCC 1137-39, 2642).

4:2 one seated: The glory of Yahweh is refracted through precious gems (4:3; 1 Tim 6:16). His throne is the focus of nearly all the activity of the book. From it come judgments (Rev 16:17; 20:11-12) and declarations of truth (21:3, 5), and around it stands an entourage of men and angels engaged in never-ending worship (4:9-10; 5:11-12; 7:9-15; 14:3; 22:3).

4:3 a rainbow: A spectrum of color encircles the divine throne. ● The rainbow, which also appears in Ezekiel's vision of the enthroned Lord (Ezek 1:28), is a sign of the Noahic covenant that God established with creation after the flood (Gen 9:8-13).

4:4 twenty-four elders: Represent the saints, who are dressed like priests (in white) and kings (with crowns). See note on Rev 1:6. ● Their number symbolizes the 24 priestly rotations that David established to minister in the Temple (1 Chron 24:1-31). In Jewish tradition, the heads of the 24 divisions were called "elders". Some see the elders representing the fullness of the royal priestly people of God: the 12 tribes of the sons of Israel (saints of the OT) plus the 12 apostles of Christ (saints of the NT), as in the vision of 21:12-14.

4:5-6 Streaks of lightning and booming thunder (4:5) feature in revelations of Yahweh's glory to Israel (Ex 19:16) and Ezekiel (Ezek 1:4, 13). The glassy sea recalls the clear sapphire pavement (Ex 24:10) and crystal flooring (Ezek 1:22) spread beneath the Lord on both occasions.

4:5 seven torches: Represent the Holy Spirit (1:4). ● The number seven recalls Zech 4:1-6, where the Spirit keeps the seven flames of the lampstand burning, and also Is 11:2,

issue flashes of lightning, and voices and peals of thunder, and before the throne burn seven torches of fire, which are the seven spirits of God; [6]and before the throne there is as it were a sea of glass, like crystal.

And round the throne, on each side of the throne, are four living creatures, full of eyes in front and behind: [7]the first living creature like a lion, the second living creature like an ox, the third living creature with the face of a man, and the fourth living creature like a flying eagle. [8]And the four living creatures, each of them with six wings, are full of eyes all round and within, and day and night they never cease to sing,

"Holy, holy, holy, is the Lord God Almighty,
who was and is and is to come!"

[9]And whenever the living creatures give glory and honor and thanks to him who is seated on the throne, who lives for ever and ever, [10]the twenty-four elders fall down before him who is seated on the throne and worship him who lives for ever and ever; they cast their crowns before the throne, singing,

[11]"Worthy are you, our Lord and God,
to receive glory and honor and power,
for you created all things,
and by your will they existed and were created."

The Scroll and the Lamb

5 And I saw in the right hand of him who was seated on the throne a scroll written within and on the back, sealed with seven seals; [2]and I saw a strong angel proclaiming with a loud voice, "Who is worthy to open the scroll and break its seals?" [3]And no one in heaven or on earth or under the earth was able to open the scroll or to look into it, [4]and I wept much that no one was found worthy to open the scroll or to look into it. [5]Then one of the elders said to me, "Weep not; behold, the Lion of the tribe of Judah, the Root of David, has conquered, so that he can open the scroll and its seven seals."

6 And between the throne and the four living creatures and among the elders, I saw a Lamb standing, as though it had been slain, with seven horns and with seven eyes, which are the seven spirits of God sent out into all the earth; [7]and he went and took the scroll from the right hand of him who was seated on the throne. [8]And when he had taken the scroll, the four living creatures and the twenty-four elders fell down before the Lamb, each holding a harp, and with golden bowls full of incense, which are the prayers of the saints; [9]and they sang a new song, saying,

"Worthy are you to take the scroll and to open
its seals,

4:6: Ezek 1:5, 18.   **4:7:** Ezek 1:10.   **4:8:** Is 6:2–3.   **4:9:** Ps 47:8.   **5:1:** Ezek 2:9; Is 29:11.
5:5: Gen 49:9.   **5:6:** Is 53:7; Zech 4:10.   **5:8:** Ps 141:2.   **5:9:** Ps 33:3.

---

where the Greek OT enumerates seven gifts of the Spirit given to the Messiah (CCC 1831).

4:6 four living creatures: Angels that appear as animals. They symbolize the glory of God expressed in creation, e.g., divine authority (lion), strength (ox), intelligence (man), and swiftness (eagle). • Their animal appearance (4:7) resembles the cherubim seen by Ezekiel (Ezek 1:10; 10:1), and their six wings (4:8) recall the seraphim seen by Isaiah (Is 6:2). • Traditional exegesis connects the four living creatures with the four evangelists. Matthew is the *man* whose Gospel begins with the human genealogy of Jesus; Mark is the roaring *lion* whose Gospel begins with the voice crying out in the wilderness; Luke is the sacrificial *ox* whose Gospel begins in the Temple; and John is the soaring *eagle* whose Gospel begins with the highest mystery of Jesus' divinity (e.g., St. Jerome, *Against Jovinianus* 1, 26). • The living creatures also refer to the whole Church. Her courage is seen in the lion, her sacrificial service in the ox, her humility in the man, and her sublimity in the flying eagle (St. Bede, *Explanation of the Apocalypse* 4, 6).

4:8 Holy, holy, holy: The *Sanctus* as chanted in the heavenly liturgy. • The hymn resembles the song of the Seraphim in Is 6:3, where the threefold repetition of "holy" is a Hebrew way of saying that Yahweh is the holiest of all (superlative degree).

5:1 scroll: A covenant document whose written decrees are put into effect in 6:1–17 and 8:1–5. • The scroll is sealed like the prophetic visions of Daniel (Dan 8:26; 12:4) and has writing on both sides like the tablets of the Decalogue (Ex 32:15) and the judgment oracles of Ezekiel (Ezek 2:9–10). Christ qualifies as the executor of the Old Covenant (Rev 5:9) with divine authority to administer its blessings and curses. • The sealed book refers to Sacred Scripture, for it was opened by no one except Christ, whose death, Resurrection, and Ascension opened access to all the mysteries it contained. None but the Lord could reveal the hidden meanings of the

sacred word (St. Gregory the Great, *Dialogues* 4, 44). **seven seals:** Wax seals prevent access to a rolled-up scroll (Is 29:11).

5:5 the Lion . . . the Root: Messianic titles for Jesus (22:16). • The first is from Gen 49:9, where the Messiah comes from Judah, the tribe symbolized by a "lion". The second is from Is 11:10, where the Messiah appears as the "root" of David's father, Jesse.

5:6 I saw a Lamb: John expects to see a Lion (5:5) but turns to see a wounded Lamb. This is the first of 28 times that Christ is depicted as a Lamb in Revelation (CCC 608, 1137). See note on Rev 5:9–10. **slain:** Christ forever appears as a sacrificial victim, having taken the scars of his Crucifixion with him into heaven (Jn 20:27). Standing upright, his posture symbolizes his victorious rising from death to life (Rev 1:18). **seven horns . . . seven eyes:** Represent the totality of power (Ps 89:17) and knowledge (Zech 4:10) possessed by Christ.

5:8 harp: Traditional accompaniment for liturgical song (Ps 33:2). **bowls full of incense:** The saints in heaven mediate the praises and petitions of the saints on earth (Rev 8:3). The rising smoke of incense is a visible sign of prayers ascending to God (Ps 141:2).

5:9–10 The Lamb receives the same worship given to the Lord God (4:11), indicating that he, too, is divine (19:10). • The words of the song recall the Exodus, when Yahweh redeemed Israel (Ex 15:13) by the shed blood of paschal lambs (Ex 12:21–27) to be a kingly and priestly nation (Ex 19:6). Here it celebrates the new Exodus accomplished by Christ, the new Passover Lamb, whose blood ransoms all nations from sin and consecrates them to serve him as a royal priesthood (Rev 1:6; 1 Pet 2:9) (CCC 608, 1546).

5:9 a new song: New songs are composed and sung every time the Lord acts in a new way to save his people (Ps 33:3; 40:3; 144:9; Is 42:10). This song is new as compared to the old victory song sung by Israel after the first Exodus (Ex 15:1–18) (CCC 2642).

for you were slain and by your blood you
 ransomed men for God
from every tribe and tongue and people and
 nation,
[10]and have made them a kingdom and priests to
 our God,
 and they shall reign on earth."
[11]Then I looked, and I heard around the throne and the living creatures and the elders the voice of many angels, numbering myriads of myriads and thousands of thousands, [12]saying with a loud voice, "Worthy is the Lamb who was slain, to receive power and wealth and wisdom and might and honor and glory and blessing!" [13]And I heard every creature in heaven and on earth and under the earth and in the sea, and all therein, saying, "To him who sits upon the throne and to the Lamb be blessing and honor and glory and might for ever and ever!" [14]And the four living creatures said, "Amen!" and the elders fell down and worshiped.

The Seven Seals

6 Now I saw when the Lamb opened one of the seven seals, and I heard one of the four living creatures say, as with a voice of thunder, "Come!" [2]And I saw, and behold, a white horse, and its rider had a bow; and a crown was given to him, and he went out conquering and to conquer.

[3] When he opened the second seal, I heard the second living creature say, "Come!" [4]And out came another horse, bright red; its rider was permitted to take peace from the earth, so that men should slay one another; and he was given a great sword.

[5] When he opened the third seal, I heard the third living creature say, "Come!" And I saw, and behold, a black horse, and its rider had a balance in his hand; [6]and I heard what seemed to be a voice in the midst of the four living creatures saying, "A quart of wheat for a denarius, [a] and three quarts of barley for a denarius; [a] but do not harm oil and wine!"

[7] When he opened the fourth seal, I heard the voice of the fourth living creature say, "Come!" [8]And I saw, and behold, a pale horse, and its rider's name was Death, and Hades followed him; and they were given power over a fourth of the earth, to kill with sword and with famine and with pestilence and by wild beasts of the earth.

[9] When he opened the fifth seal, I saw under the altar the souls of those who had been slain for the word of God and for the witness they had borne; [10]they cried out with a loud voice, "O Sovereign Lord, holy and true, how long before you will judge and avenge our blood on those who dwell upon the earth?" [11]Then they were each given a white robe and told to rest a little longer, until the number of

---

5:10: Ex 19:6; Is 61:6.   **5:11:** Dan 7:10.   **6:2:** Zech 1:8; 6:1–3.   **6:6:** 2 Kings 6:25.
   6:8: Hos 13:14; Ezek 5:12.   **6:10:** Zech 1:12; Ps 79:5; Gen 4:10.

5:11 myriads of myriads: Countless angels gather to praise the Lord (Dan 7:10) and the Lamb (Heb 1:6).

6:1—8:5 The breaking of the seals brings judgment upon the earth, which is stained with the righteous blood of the martyrs (6:11). These judgments parallel the eschatological woes that Jesus warned would lead up to the fall of Jerusalem: wars (6:2; Lk 21:9), international strife (6:4; Lk 21:10), famine (6:6; Lk 21:11), pestilence (6:8; Lk 21:11), persecution (6:9; Lk 21:12), earthquakes (6:12; Lk 21:11), and cosmic disturbances (6:12–14; Lk 21:25–26). History tells of an explosion of warfare, calamities, and upheaval in the years leading up to A.D. 70 and the final devastation of the city. ● Conquest, sword, famine, pestilence, and wild beasts (6:2, 4, 8) are forms of the sevenfold covenant curse stipulated in the Torah (Lev 26:14–26). Though devastating, these catastrophes are merely a prelude to the worst judgment of all—the utter devastation of the land of Israel and the dispersion of its survivors (Lev 26:27–33). This sevenfold vengeance of Yahweh is also the backdrop for the seven trumpets (Rev 8:6—11:19) and the seven bowls of wrath (Rev 15:1—16:21).

6:1-8 The vision of the four horsemen. Each one symbolizes the divine judgment he is authorized to execute, whether it be conquest (white horse), bloodshed (red horse), famine (black horse), or death (pale horse). ● The vision draws from Zech 1:8-17 and 6:1-8, where four chariots with colored horses patrol the earth after the Babylonian conquest of Israel in 586 B.C. Here the events that ensue are strangely reversed: Zechariah announced an end to the punishment of Israel, but Revelation envisions a new beginning of divine chastisement.

6:6 denarius: A full day's wage (Mt 20:2) buys only a day's ration of wheat for one person and a ration of barley for a small family. Limited food supplies and inflated prices are sure signs of famine. **oil and wine:** Crops harvested in late summer (olives and grapes) are not to be devastated like the crops harvested in late spring (wheat and barley). A limit is set, lest the famine continue into the next harvest season.

6:8 Death . . . Hades: Personify the satanic forces that bring death and destruction into the world. Both are under the authority of Christ, who conquered them by his rising (1:18) and doomed them to everlasting destruction (20:13-14). **sword . . . famine . . . pestilence . . . beasts:** The judgments of the fourth horsemen. ● The same four curses ravaged Jerusalem in the sixth century B.C. (Ezek 14:21) as punishment for its infidelity to the Lord (Deut 32:23-25).

6:9 the altar: The heavenly counterpart to the bronze altar of sacrifice in the Jerusalem Temple (2 Chron 4:1). **slain for the word** The martyrs bear the likeness of Christ, the slain Lamb (12:11; Mt 23:34-35). Their pleas for justice sound from beneath the altar, recalling how the lifeblood (Lev 17:11) of sacrificial victims was poured out at the base of the Temple altar (Lev 4:7). Martyrdom is thus portrayed as a priestly act of sacrificing one's life to God (Rom 12:1; Phil 2:17; 1 Pet 2:5).

6:10 how long: The martyrs long for God to redress their murders. ● They pray, not out of hatred for their enemies, but out of love for justice. Being near the Judge, they agree with him and pray for the coming judgment, in which the reign of sin shall be destroyed and their lifeless bodies raised (St. Bede, *Explanation of the Apocalypse* 6, 10) (CCC 2817).

6:11 white robe: Symbolic of victory and spiritual purity (3:5; 7:9, 14). White vestments were also worn by the high priests of Israel. See note on Rev 3:4. **should be complete:** Jewish tradition spoke of a quota of martyrs determined in advance by God (*1 Enoch* 47, 1-4).

---

[a] The denarius was a day's wage for a laborer.

their fellow servants and their brethren should be complete, who were to be killed as they themselves had been.

12 When he opened the sixth seal, I looked, and behold, there was a great earthquake; and the sun became black as sackcloth, the full moon became like blood, [13]and the stars of the sky fell to the earth as the fig tree sheds its winter fruit when shaken by a gale; [14]the sky vanished like a scroll that is rolled up, and every mountain and island was removed from its place. [15]Then the kings of the earth and the great men and the generals and the rich and the strong, and every one, slave and free, hid in the caves and among the rocks of the mountains, [16]calling to the mountains and rocks, "Fall on us and hide us from the face of him who is seated on the throne, and from the wrath of the Lamb; [17]for the great day of their wrath has come, and who can stand before it?"

The 144,000 of Israel Sealed

7 After this I saw four angels standing at the four corners of the earth, holding back the four winds of the earth, that no wind might blow on earth or sea or against any tree. [2]Then I saw an-other angel ascend from the rising of the sun, with the seal of the living God, and he called with a loud voice to the four angels who had been given power to harm earth and sea, [3]saying, "Do not harm the earth or the sea or the trees, till we have sealed the servants of our God upon their foreheads." [4]And I heard the number of the sealed, a hundred and forty-four thousand sealed, out of every tribe of the sons of Israel, [5]twelve thousand sealed out of the tribe of Judah, twelve thousand of the tribe of Reuben, twelve thousand of the tribe of Gad, [6]twelve thousand of the tribe of Asher, twelve thousand of the tribe of Naph′tali, twelve thousand of the tribe of Manas′seh, [7]twelve thousand of the tribe of Simeon, twelve thousand of the tribe of Levi, twelve thousand of the tribe of Is′sachar, [8]twelve thousand of the tribe of Zeb′ulun, twelve thousand of the tribe of Joseph, twelve thousand sealed out of the tribe of Benjamin.

The Multitude from Every Nation

9 After this I looked, and behold, a great multitude which no man could number, from every nation, from all tribes and peoples and tongues, standing before the throne and before the Lamb,

---

6:12: Joel 2:31; Acts 2:20.   6:13: Is 34:4.   6:15: Is 2:10.   6:16: Hos 10:8.
6:17: Joel 2:11; Mal 3:2.   7:1: Zech 6:5.   7:3: Ezek 9:4.

6:12–14 Scenes of apocalyptic disaster may be understood literally, as describing the end of the world and the consummation of history (2 Pet 3:10–13), or symbolically, as representing spiritual and political upheaval within history (Is 13:10–13; 34:4; 50:3; Joel 2:30–32; Hag 2:21–22). Though a literal fulfillment cannot be ruled out for the future, the woes unleashed by the seven seals are parallel to the eschatological woes that Jesus warned would seize the world just before the Roman conquest of Jerusalem in A.D. 70 (see Lk 21:5–28).

6:15 kings . . . and free Judgment will fall on men of every rank. **hid in the caves:** Recalls the sinners in Is 2:19, who hide themselves in caves from the terror of God's majesty.

6:16 Fall on us . . . hide us: Cries of distress from those engulfed in the tribulation seizing the world. See note on Rev 3:10. ● These cries come from Hos 10:8, where the people of Samaria groan in travail over the violent destruction of their city. On one occasion, Jesus put Hosea's words on the lips of those doomed to witness the overthrow of Jerusalem (Lk 23:28–30).

6:17 who can stand: Standing is a sign of vindication on the Day of Judgment (Dan 12:13; Eph 6:13). The Lamb (Rev 5:6), the angels (7:11), and the saints (7:9) all appear in this posture in Revelation. ● Passages such as Nahum 1:6 and Mal 3:2 indicate that the question "Who can stand?" is rhetorical, implying that no sinner can hope to stand before the wrath of the divine Judge.

7:1–17 Chapter 7 is an interlude that follows the sixth seal and delays the opening of the seventh, just as 10:1–11:14 is an interlude that follows the sixth trumpet and delays the blowing of the seventh. John sees the remnant of Israel (7:1–8) and the saved of all nations (7:9–17).

7:1 the four corners: Perhaps the earth is pictured as a four-cornered altar (cf. 9:13) upon which the martyrs shed their blood in sacrifice (6:9–11).

7:3 sealed: A seal is a mark of ownership and protection (9:4). Here the seal of God is related to the seals of the scroll, giving protection to the believing remnant of Israel, who will pass through the tribulation. This may refer to a grace of spiritual perseverance rather than a guarantee of physical survival. In the broader context of Revelation, there is a contrast between the *seal* of God stamped on the foreheads of the righteous (7:2) and the *mark* of the beast inscribed on the brows of the wicked (13:16). The former bears the divine name of God (14:1; 22:4), while the latter bears the demonic name of the beast (13:17) (CCC 1296). See note on 2 Cor 1:22. ● The entire scene parallels Ezek 9:1–7, where a messenger seals the foreheads of the righteous in Israel to protect them from the wrath of God poured out on Jerusalem. The seal was shaped like the Hebrew letter *taw*, which in ancient script looked like a cross (× or +). Marks of divine protection can be traced as far back as Cain in Gen 4:15.

7:4 a hundred and forty-four thousand: The number of the tribes of Israel squared (12 × 12) and then multiplied by a thousand, signifying completeness (144 × 1000).

7:5–8 Two irregularities stand out in the enumeration of the twelve tribes. **(1)** The tribe of Judah heads the list, even though Judah was the fourth son of Jacob. The descent of Christ from Judah probably accounts for this (5:5; Mt 1:2–16). **(2)** The tribe of Dan is missing. It is possible that Dan was cut from the list because of the tribe's infamous love for idolatry (Judg 18:16–19). Others suggest that John is following an ancient tradition that held that the Antichrist would come from Dan. Whatever the reason for the omission, Israel was technically a family of 13 tribes (the tribe of Joseph splitting into the tribes of Ephraim and Manasseh, Gen 48:1–20), and so one of the tribes had to be dropped to keep the symbolism of the number 12 intact (Rev 21:12).

7:9 a great multitude: The saints in heaven who passed through the great tribulation without compromising their faith (7:14). **no man could number:** The uncountable throng represents the spiritual offspring of Abraham, i.e., those who imitated his faith (Rom 4:11–17). ● The Lord had promised to make Abraham the father of many nations (Gen 17:5) and to give him progeny too numerous to count (Gen 15:5). **white robes:** The garments of the faithful who endured the purifying trials of tribulation (Dan 11:35; 12:10). See note on Rev 3:4. **palm branches:** Waved at the annual Feast of Tabernacles (Booths) in the liturgy of ancient Israel (Lev 23:40; 2 Mac 10:6–7). ● The international celebration of Tabernacles has its background in Zech 14:16.

clothed in white robes, with palm branches in their hands, [10]and crying out with a loud voice, "Salvation belongs to our God who sits upon the throne, and to the Lamb!" [11]And all the angels stood round the throne and round the elders and the four living creatures, and they fell on their faces before the throne and worshiped God, [12]saying, "Amen! Blessing and glory and wisdom and thanksgiving and honor and power and might be to our God for ever and ever! Amen."

13 Then one of the elders addressed me, saying, "Who are these, clothed in white robes, and from where have they come?" [14]I said to him, "Sir, you know." And he said to me, "These are they who have come out of the great tribulation; they have washed their robes and made them white in the blood of the Lamb.

[15]Therefore are they before the throne of God,
and serve him day and night within his
temple;
and he who sits upon the throne will shelter
them with his presence.

[16]They shall hunger no more, neither thirst any
more;
the sun shall not strike them, nor any
scorching heat.
[17]For the Lamb in the midst of the throne will be
their shepherd,
and he will guide them to springs of living
water;
and God will wipe away every tear from their
eyes."

The Seventh Seal and the Golden Censer

8 When the Lamb opened the seventh seal, there was silence in heaven for about half an hour. [2]Then I saw the seven angels who stand before God, and seven trumpets were given to them. [3]And another angel came and stood at the altar with a golden censer; and he was given much incense to mingle with the prayers of all the saints upon the golden altar before the throne; [4]and the smoke of the incense rose with the prayers of the saints from the hand of the angel before God. [5]Then the angel took the censer and filled it with fire from

---

7:14: Dan 12:1; Gen 49:11.   **7:16:** Is 49:10; Ps 121:6.   **7:17:** Ezek 34:23; Ps 23:2; Is 25:8.
8:3: Amos 9:1; Ps 141:2.   **8:5:** Lev 16:12; Ezek 10:2.

7:12 Blessing . . . and might: The seven acclamations signify that God deserves the totality of praise from his creation.

7:14 great tribulation: A time of unprecedented distress triggered by the opening of the seals (6:1–17; Dan 12:1). Some link this with the "great tribulation" that Jesus warned would engulf the Roman world in connection with the violent conquest of Jerusalem (Mt 24:21); others link it with the Domitianic persecution of Christians near the end of the first century. See note on Rev 3:10. **they have washed:** The blood of Christ whitens the robes of the saints (6:11). ● The rite of priestly ordination in Israel included the purification of priestly garments with blood (Lev 8:30). The sacrificial blood of Jesus

Word Study

Shelter (Rev 7:15)

Skēnoō (Gk.): a verb meaning "to dwell" or "pitch a tent". It appears once in the Gospel of John and four times in Revelation. Its usage is inspired by memories of the Tabernacle pitched in the wilderness during the Exodus period. For a time, this large tent served as the place where Yahweh dwelt among the people of Israel (Ex 25:8; Lev 26:11). From John's perspective, the Tabernacle was a prophetic sign of the incarnate Christ, whose humanity is a sanctuary filled with the glory of his divinity (Jn 1:14). Revelation uses the verb to describe God spreading a tent of protection over the saints (Rev 7:15) so that he might dwell with them (Rev 21:3) and they in him (Rev 13:6; cf. 21:22). Thus, the same verb that expresses the mystery of God dwelling on earth in the Gospel of John (bodily sanctuary) also expresses the mystery of God's dwelling on high in Revelation (heavenly sanctuary).

likewise consecrates believers for service in the heavenly temple (5:9–10; 7:15).

7:15–17 The unending benefits of heaven. ● These blessings correspond to Isaiah's visions of the messianic age: God's sheltering presence (Is 4:5–6), immunity to hunger, thirst, and heat (Is 49:10), and the divine consolation that wipes away every tear (Is 25:8).

7:15 his temple: The heavenly sanctuary of God (11:19). See note on Rev 4:1—5:14.

8:1 silence in heaven: Recalls the *liturgical* silence that fell over the Jerusalem Temple when the priests offered incense and the multitudes prayed quietly in the outer courts (Lk 1:8–10). Jewish tradition also speaks of an *angelic* silence in the heaven when Israel prays and when the judgments of God are about to fall (Hab 2:20; Zeph 1:7). Here an angel offers the prayers of the saints with incense (Rev 8:3–4) just before curses descend upon the earth (8:7–9:21; 11:15–19).

8:2 the seven angels: Seven archangels minister in the presence of God according to Scripture (Tob 12:15) and Jewish tradition, which names them Uriel, Raphael, Raguel, Michael, Saraqael, Gabriel, and Remiel (*1 Enoch* 20, 1–8; 81, 5). They are known as the angels of the Lord's presence (*Testament of Levi* 3, 7; cf. Lk 1:19).

8:3 prayers of all the saints: Like priests on earth, the angels in heaven are liturgical ministers as well as covenant mediators between God and his people. They are vested like priests according to 15:6, and here they offer as incense the petitions of the faithful. The company of *all* the saints probably includes those in heaven, such as the martyrs (6:9–11) and the multitudes (7:13–14) who praise God for his mercy and plead for the judgment of the wicked. ● The Communion of the Saints is the basis for the intercession of the saints. Just as the faithful pray for one another on earth, so the faithful departed pray for us as they look down from heaven (CCC 954–56). **the golden altar:** The heavenly counterpart to the altar of incense in the Temple (2 Chron 4:19; Lk 1:11). See note on Rev 4:1—5:14.

8:5 threw it on the earth: An act of divine judgment on the earth. ● The gesture recalls Ezek 10:2, where a heavenly messenger scatters burning coals over Jerusalem.

the altar and threw it on the earth; and there were peals of thunder, loud noises, flashes of lightning, and an earthquake.

The Seven Angels and Seven Trumpets

6 Now the seven angels who had the seven trumpets made ready to blow them.

7 The first angel blew his trumpet, and there followed hail and fire, mixed with blood, which fell on the earth; and a third of the earth was burnt up, and a third of the trees were burnt up, and all green grass was burnt up.

8 The second angel blew his trumpet, and something like a great mountain, burning with fire, was thrown into the sea; [9]and a third of the sea became blood, a third of the living creatures in the sea died, and a third of the ships were destroyed.

10 The third angel blew his trumpet, and a great star fell from heaven, blazing like a torch, and it fell on a third of the rivers and on the fountains of water. [11]The name of the star is Wormwood. A third of the waters became wormwood, and many men died of the water, because it was made bitter.

12 The fourth angel blew his trumpet, and a third of the sun was struck, and a third of the moon, and a third of the stars, so that a third of their light was darkened; a third of the day was kept from shining, and likewise a third of the night.

13 Then I looked, and I heard an eagle crying with a loud voice, as it flew in midheaven, "Woe, woe, woe to those who dwell on the earth, at the blasts of the other trumpets which the three angels are about to blow!"

9 And the fifth angel blew his trumpet, and I saw a star fallen from heaven to earth, and he was given the key of the shaft of the bottomless pit; [2]he opened the shaft of the bottomless pit, and from the shaft rose smoke like the smoke of a great furnace, and the sun and the air were darkened with the smoke from the shaft. [3]Then from the smoke came locusts on the earth, and they were given power like the power of scorpions of the earth; [4]they were told not to harm the grass of the earth or any green growth or any tree, but only those of mankind who have not the seal of God upon their foreheads; [5]they were allowed to torture them for five months, but not to kill them, and their torture was like the torture of a scorpion, when it stings a man. [6]And in those days men will seek death and will not find it; they will long to die, and death will fly from them.

7 In appearance the locusts were like horses arrayed for battle; on their heads were what looked like crowns of gold; their faces were like human faces, [8]their hair like women's hair, and their teeth like lions' teeth; [9]they had scales like iron breastplates, and the noise of their wings was like the noise of many chariots with horses rushing into battle. [10]They have tails like scorpions, and stings, and their power of hurting men for five months lies in their tails. [11]They have as king over them the angel of the bottomless pit; his name in Hebrew is Abad´don, and in Greek he is called Apol´lyon. [b]

12 The first woe has passed; behold, two woes are still to come.

8:7: Ex 9:23–25. **8:8:** Jer 51:25. **8:10:** Is 14:12. **9:2:** Gen 19:28; Ex 19:18; Joel 2:10.
9:3: Ex 10:12–15. **9:4:** Ezek 9:4. **9:6:** Job 3:21. **9:7:** Joel 2:4. **9:8:** Joel 1:6. **9:9:** Joel 2:5.

8:7—11:19 The seven trumpets blast the earth with sevenfold judgment. The second of three cycles of chastisement in Revelation, the trumpets wreak havoc more severe than the seven seals (6:1—8:5) but less severe than the following seven bowls (16:1–21). See note on Rev 6:1—8:5. ● The first four trumpets, which devastate a third of the land, sea, freshwater, and sky, are modeled on the Exodus plagues that ravaged Egypt: recall the fiery **hail** (8:7, seventh plague, Ex 9:23–25), the sea made **blood** (8:9, first plague, Ex 7:20–21), the **darkened** sky (8:12, ninth plague, Ex 10:21–23), and the **locusts** (9:3, eighth plague, Ex 10:12–15).

8:11 Wormwood: The name of a bitter plant that symbolizes the sorrow and distaste of human affliction (Jer 9:15; Lam 3:19). **made bitter:** I.e., undrinkable. ● This plague recalls but reverses the story in Ex 15:22–25, where God made the bitter waters sweet.

8:13 Woe, woe, woe: A prophetic warning that judgment is about to rain down upon sinners (Is 5:8–23; Amos 5:18; Nahum 3:1). These woes correspond to the plagues unleashed by the final three trumpets (Rev 9:12; 11:14).

9:1–12 The fifth trumpet unlocks the abyss, releasing volcanic smoke and swarms of warrior locusts. These are demonic forces let loose to torture and terrorize the earth. Four restrictions are placed on this first woe: **(1)** vegetation is to be left unharmed (9:4); **(2)** only the wicked are to be targeted for torment (9:4); **(3)** victims are not to be killed (9:5); and **(4)** the

plague is to end in five months (9:5). Limitations such as these suggest that God is administering remedial or corrective punishment that is aimed at bringing about repentance (9:20–21). ● The prophet Joel once described an invasion of locusts that overran Judea in OT times. As in John's vision, he compared them to an army of war horses (9:7; Joel 2:4) with lion's teeth (9:8; Joel 1:6) and wings that sounded like chariots (9:9; Joel 2:5). This, too, was a plague from the Lord intended to induce repentance (Joel 2:12–16).

9:1 a star fallen: A demon or fallen angel (8:10; 12:4, 9). **the bottomless pit:** Or "the abyss", which corresponds to the Hebrew *Sheol* and the Greek *Hades*. In the cosmology of Israel, this is the gloomy underworld where the spirits of men sink down after death to await the final Judgment (20:13; Ps 9:17; Wis 16:13–14). It is also the dwelling of infernal spirits that crawl up to bring death, destruction, and deception into the world of the living (11:7; 20:1–3; Lk 8:29–31; 2 Pet 2:4). Christ has authority over this realm because he holds the "keys" to the abyss and can order angels and demons to lock and unlock it at his discretion (1:18; 20:1).

9:4 the seal of God: A mark of protection on the righteous of Israel. See note on Rev 7:3.

9:5 five months: Roughly equivalent to the life cycle of an actual locust.

9:11 his name: *Abaddon* is a Hebrew term that means "destruction", and *Apollyon* is a Greek term that means "destroyer". ● The former is associated with the underworld in Job 26:6, Ps 88:11, and Prov 15:11.

---

[b] Or *Destroyer*.

13 Then the sixth angel blew his trumpet, and I heard a voice from the four horns of the golden altar before God, [14]saying to the sixth angel who had the trumpet, "Release the four angels who are bound at the great river Euphra´tes." [15]So the four angels were released, who had been held ready for the hour, the day, the month, and the year, to kill a third of mankind. [16]The number of the troops of cavalry was twice ten thousand times ten thousand; I heard their number. [17]And this was how I saw the horses in my vision: the riders wore breastplates the color of fire and of sapphire [c] and of sulphur, and the heads of the horses were like lions' heads, and fire and smoke and sulphur issued from their mouths. [18]By these three plagues a third of mankind was killed, by the fire and smoke and sulphur issuing from their mouths. [19]For the power of the horses is in their mouths and in their tails; their tails are like serpents, with heads, and by means of them they wound.

20 The rest of mankind, who were not killed by these plagues, did not repent of the works of their hands nor give up worshiping demons and idols of gold and silver and bronze and stone and wood, which cannot either see or hear or walk; [21]nor did they repent of their murders or their sorceries or their immorality or their thefts.

The Angel with the Little Scroll

10 Then I saw another mighty angel coming down from heaven, wrapped in a cloud, with a rainbow over his head, and his face was like the sun, and his legs like pillars of fire. [2]He had a little scroll open in his hand. And he set his right foot on the sea, and his left foot on the land, [3]and called out with a loud voice, like a lion roaring; when he called out, the seven thunders sounded. [4]And when the seven thunders had sounded, I was about to write, but I heard a voice from heaven saying, "Seal up what the seven thunders have said, and do not write it down." [5]And the angel whom I saw standing on sea and land lifted up his right hand to heaven [6]and swore by him who lives for ever and ever, who created heaven and what is in it, the earth and what is in it, and the sea and what is in it, that there should be no more delay, [7]but that in the days of the trumpet call to be sounded by the seventh angel, the mystery of God, as he announced to his servants the prophets, should be fulfilled.

8 Then the voice which I had heard from heaven spoke to me again, saying, "Go, take the scroll which is open in the hand of the angel who is standing on the sea and on the land." [9]So I went to the angel and told him to give me the little scroll; and he said to me, "Take it and eat; it will be bitter

---

9:13: Ex 30:1–3.   **9:20:** Is 17:8; Ps 115:4–7; 135:15–17.   **10:5:** Deut 32:40; Dan 12:7.
10:9: Ezek 2:8; 3:1–3.

9:13–21 The sixth trumpet unbinds four demons who rouse an army of fire-breathing horses into battle. Unlike the locusts (9:5), these beasts with lion heads and serpent tails are given permission to kill masses of human life (9:18).

9:13 the golden altar: The heavenly altar of incense, where the prayers of the saints ascend before God (8:3). Like its earthly counterpart, it has four horns protruding from its four corners (Ex 37:25–28).

9:14 river Euphrates: The longest river in ancient Mesopotamia. Along its banks lived the Babylonians, one of the traditional archenemies of Israel.

9:15 hour . . . day . . . month . . . year: The plan of God unfolds according to a precise timetable determined in advance. **a third of mankind:** The same fraction is applied to the plagues unleashed by the earlier trumpets (8:7, 9–10, 12).

9:20 did not repent: The survivors of the sixth trumpet remain hardened in their wickedness (16:9, 11) despite the merciful purpose of these judgments to discipline sinners and bring them back to God (Lev 26:14–33). **worshiping demons and idols:** The Bible equates idolatry with service to fallen spirits (Deut 32:16–17; Ps 106:36–37). Taunts against idols as lifeless and motionless images were proverbial (Ps 115:4–7; Dan 5:23; Hab 2:18–19).

10:1—11:14 An interlude separates the sixth (9:13–21) and seventh trumpet (11:15–19), just as an interlude separated the sixth and seventh seal (7:1–17). This one sets in motion the second half of the book by renewing the commission to John, charged at the beginning of the book with writing down the prophetic visions (1:11), to prophesy "again" (10:11).

10:1–11 An enormous angel descends to earth, its legs straddling the shoreline and its right arm raised to swear an oath. Its appearance radiates the glory of the Father (rainbow, 4:3), the Son (wrapped in clouds, 1:7; face like the sun, 1:16), and the Holy Spirit (pillars of fire, Ex 13:21).

Perhaps this is the Lord's angel who conveys to John the revelations of the book (1:1; 22:6). ● Elsewhere in Scripture the "angel of the Lord" swears an oath in the name of God (Gen 22:15–18) and commissions both Prophets and Judges (Ex 3:2–10; Judg 6:11–14; 1 Chron 21:18). The immediate background is Dan 10–12, where Daniel encounters a heavenly figure who stood over the Tigris River. This messenger, too, had a glorious appearance (Dan 10:5–6) and swore an oath that God's plan would be fulfilled in the future (Dan 12:7). John stands at the other end of this prophetic pledge: what was far distant in Daniel's day is fast approaching in his own (10:6). ● The angel takes an oath, not because of any defect in himself, as if one could not trust his word, but in order to show that his utterance proceeds from an infallible ordinance of God (St. Thomas Aquinas, *Summa Theologiae* II–II, 89, 10).

10:1 another mighty angel: Distinct from the first "strong angel" (5:2) who cried out in a "loud voice" (10:3).

10:2 little scroll: Seemingly a different scroll from that in 5:1 (the Greek terms are different).

10:3 a lion roaring: The angel speaks the words of Christ, the Lion of Judah (5:5; cf. Is 31:4; Hos 11:10; Amos 3:8). **seven thunders:** The mighty voice of the Lord (Ps 29:3–9). It may be linked with the Spirit, who earlier appears as "seven spirits" (1:4) and "seven torches" (4:5).

10:6 swore by him: The posture of the angel (10:5) is related to the oath: his hand touches heaven, and his feet span land and sea when he swears to the Creator of heaven, earth, and sea. Raising the hand is one of many gestures connected with oath swearing in the biblical world (Deut 32:40).

10:7 the mystery of God: Unveiled as the kingdom of God that comes with the blast of the seventh trumpet (11:15). ● The link between "mystery" and the messianic "kingdom" is forged in Daniel (Dan 2:28, 44–47; 7:13–14).

10:9 Take it and eat: A renewal of John's prophetic mission to speak the word of God (10:11). The message he receives is sweet because it promises hope but turns sour

---

[c] Greek *hyacinth.*

to your stomach, but sweet as honey in your mouth." [10]And I took the little scroll from the hand of the angel and ate it; it was sweet as honey in my mouth, but when I had eaten it my stomach was made bitter. [11]And I was told, "You must again prophesy about many peoples and nations and tongues and kings."

The Two Witnesses

11 Then I was given a measuring rod like a staff, and I was told: "Rise and measure the temple of God and the altar and those who worship there, [2]but do not measure the court outside the temple; leave that out, for it is given over to the nations, and they will trample over the holy city for forty-two months. [3]And I will grant my two wit-

nesses power to prophesy for one thousand two hundred and sixty days, clothed in sackcloth."

4 These are the two olive trees and the two lampstands which stand before the Lord of the earth. [5]And if any one would harm them, fire pours from their mouth and consumes their foes; if any one would harm them, thus he is doomed to be killed. [6]They have power to shut the sky, that no rain may fall during the days of their prophesying, and they have power over the waters to turn them into blood, and to afflict the earth with every plague, as often as they desire. [7]And when they have finished their testimony, the beast that ascends from the bottomless pit will make war upon them and conquer them and kill them, [8]and their dead bodies will lie

---

10:11: Jer 1:10.   **11:1:** Ezek 40:3.   **11:2:** Zech 12:3; Is 63:18; Lk 21:24.   **11:4:** Zech 4:3, 11–14.
11:5: 2 Kings 1:10; Jer 5:14.   **11:6:** 1 Kings 17:1; Ex 7:17, 19.   **11:7:** Dan 7:3, 7, 21.
11:8: Is 1:9.

---

because it entails suffering for saints and sinners alike. • The scene is modeled on Ezek 2:8—3:3, where the prophet consumed a scroll inscribed with judgments against Israel. At first, the scroll was sweet (Ezek 3:3), but its words of lamentation and woe made his task a bitter one (Ezek 3:14).

10:11 again prophesy: John is to prophesy what is recorded in the visions of chaps. 11–22.

11:1 measure the temple: A prophetic action in which John measures the sanctuary with a reed but excludes the outer court. There is broad agreement that his action is symbolic and that a spiritual distinction is implied, e.g., believing Israel (or believers in general) is marked out for protection, while unbelieving Israel (or unbelievers in general) is given over to judgment. The *measuring* that precedes the seventh trumpet (11:15) thus parallels the *sealing* that took place before the seventh seal (7:1–8). There is less agreement over what is measured. Some take it to be the Herodian Temple in Jerusalem, which was encompassed by an outer courtyard called the Court of the Gentiles. Others note that John elsewhere speaks of the temple of God in heaven (11:19; 14:17; 15:5), in which case the trampling of the outer court may symbolize the Church being persecuted by the unbelieving world. • Measuring the dimensions of the temple with a reed draws on imagery from Ezek 40–42.

11:2 trample over the holy city: Taken literally, this would refer to the Roman conquest of Jerusalem in A.D. 70, as in Lk 21:24. Though mass numbers of Jews perished in the calamity, the Christians of Jerusalem fled safely to the Transjordan town of Pella (Lk 21:20–21; Eusebius, *Ecclesiastical History* 3, 5). Taken symbolically, this could refer to the persecution of the saints, whose destiny is the holy city above (Rev 21:2, 10). • Jerusalem and its sanctuary were twice before trampled down by the Gentiles, once by the Babylonians (Is 63:18) and then again by the Syrians (1 Mac 3:45). **forty-two months:** A time of tribulation (13:5), also described as three and a half years (12:14) or 1,260 days (11:3; 12:6). Some interpret these figures literally; others read them figuratively, indicating a limited period of persecution or as representing the entire course of Church history. • The time frame is drawn from Daniel's vision of a tribulation to come upon the People of God in the future (Dan 7:25; 9:27; 12:7). This was foreshadowed by the Syrian desecration of Jerusalem from 167 to 164 B.C.

11:3 two witnesses: Represent the Church's witness to Israel and, more specifically, her conviction that the Law and the Prophets bear witness to Christ. So understood, the fate of the two witnesses symbolize the rejection of the gospel by unbelieving Israel (11:10), as well as the Church's confor-

mity to Christ in his dying, rising, and exaltation (11:7, 11–12). Some see the witnesses as two historical individuals, either as two unknown martyrs or as two figures from the OT, such as Moses and Elijah or Enoch and Elijah. • The actions of the witnesses recall those of Moses and Elijah: they "shut the sky" (11:6; 1 Kings 17:1); they turn water "into blood" (11:6; Ex 7:20); they are taken up to "heaven" (11:12; 2 Kings 2:11); and they give "testimony" to Jesus (11:7; Lk 9:28–31). **sackcloth:** A coarse garment of goat hair worn as a sign of mourning and repentance (Dan 9:3; Joel 1:13).

11:4 two olive trees: An image drawn from Zech 4:1–14. • Zechariah saw two olive trees that symbolized the anointed leaders of Israel who helped to rebuild the nation after the Babylonian exile: the royal governor Zerubbabel and the high priest Joshua. Here they represent the twofold mission of the Church to be a royal and priestly witness to the gospel (1:6; 5:10).

11:7 the beast: Later mentioned in 13:1 and 17:8.

11:8 the great city: The city of Jerusalem (Jer 22:8), which crucified the Lord Jesus and took the lives of numerous early Christians (Acts 5:28–30; 7:58–60; 12:2; 26:10).

Word Study

Witnesses (Rev 11:3)

Martys (Gk.): a noun meaning "witness". The term is used in a variety of ways in the NT. **(1)** In a legal sense, a witness is "one who testifies" before a court or panel of authorities (Acts 6:13; 2 Cor 13:1; 1 Tim 5:19). **(2)** A witness can be an "eyewitness", referring to one who has seen or heard something and who may be called upon to vouch for it (Acts 22:15; 1 Thess 2:10). Paul invokes God in this way as a witness to his intentions and interior actions (Rom 1:9; 2 Cor 1:23). **(3)** A witness can be a "messenger". In this sense, the apostles are witnesses who tell the world of the dying and rising of Jesus (Acts 1:8, 22; 10:39). **(4)** In early Christian times, the word acquired the specialized meaning of "martyr", referring to someone who testifies to Christ to the point of death (Acts 22:20). This is the sense of the term in Revelation, where Jesus is the prototype of the martyrs (Rev 1:5; 3:14) who choose to die for him rather than deny him and his gospel (Rev 2:13; 11:3; 17:6).

---

a Greek *spiritually*.

in the street of the great city which is allegorically[d] called Sodom and Egypt, where their Lord was crucified. [9]For three days and a half men from the peoples and tribes and tongues and nations gaze at their dead bodies and refuse to let them be placed in a tomb, [10]and those who dwell on the earth will rejoice over them and make merry and exchange presents, because these two prophets had been a torment to those who dwell on the earth. [11]But after the three and a half days a breath of life from God entered them, and they stood up on their feet, and great fear fell on those who saw them. [12]Then they heard a loud voice from heaven saying to them, "Come up here!" And in the sight of their foes they went up to heaven in a cloud. [13]And at that hour there was a great earthquake, and a tenth of the city fell; seven thousand people were killed in the earthquake, and the rest were terrified and gave glory to the God of heaven.

14 The second woe has passed; behold, the third woe is soon to come.

The Seventh Trumpet

15 Then the seventh angel blew his trumpet, and there were loud voices in heaven, saying, "The kingdom of the world has become the king-dom of our Lord and of his Christ, and he shall reign for ever and ever." [16]And the twenty-four elders who sit on their thrones before God fell on their faces and worshiped God, [17]saying,

"We give thanks to you, Lord God Almighty,
      who are and who were,
      that you have taken your great power and
         begun to reign.
[18]The nations raged, but your wrath came,
      and the time for the dead to be judged,
      for rewarding your servants, the prophets and
         saints,
      and those who fear your name, both small and
         great,
   and for destroying the destroyers of the earth."

19 Then God's temple in heaven was opened, and the ark of his covenant was seen within his temple; and there were flashes of lightning, loud noises, peals of thunder, an earthquake, and heavy hail.

The Woman and the Dragon

12 And a great sign appeared in heaven, a woman clothed with the sun, with the moon under her feet, and on her head a crown of twelve stars; [2]she was with child and she cried out in her

---

11:11: Ezek 37:5, 10.   **11:12:** 2 Kings 2:11.   **11:15:** Ps 22:28; Dan 7:14, 27.   **11:18:** Ps 2:1.
11:19: 1 Kings 8:1–6; 2 Mac 2:4–8.   **12:2:** Mic 4:10.

Some interpret this verse figuratively as a reference to the unbelieving world and its hostility toward the Church. This is the first of several references to the "great city" in Revelation (17:18; 18:10, 16, 18, 19, 21). **Sodom and Egypt:** Places infamous in the Bible for their moral depravity and oppressive slavery (Gen 18:20; Ex 1:8–14). ● Occasionally the Prophets compared the iniquity of Jerusalem to that of Sodom and Egypt (Is 3:9; Jer 23:14; Ezek 23:27).

11:9 men from the peoples: The Gentiles in general or perhaps Diaspora Jews living among them throughout the Roman world. The world applauds Jerusalem's violent attempt to halt the advance of the gospel.

11:11 breath of life: An allusion to Ezek 37:1–14, where the restoration of faithful Israel is portrayed as a resurrection of bodies by the breath of the Spirit.

11:12 in a cloud: Recalls how Jesus ascended to heaven in a cloud (Acts 1:9) and anticipates how the saints, too, will ascend into glory after the general resurrection (1 Thess 4:16–17).

11:13 earthquake: The murderous city experiences the first tremor of divine judgment. **tenth of the city:** The figure of 7,000 casualties, indicative of sevenfold judgment, suggests Jerusalem is still in view. See note on Rev 6:1–8:5. **gave glory:** This is the only chastisement in Revelation that leads some to repentance (contrast with 9:20–21 and 16:9, 11).

11:14 the third woe: The seventh trumpet (11:15). See note on Rev 8:13.

11:15–19 The seventh trumpet, which ends the second series of judgments delayed since 10:1. With this final blast, the kingdom of Christ appears, judgment begins, and destruction overtakes the wicked. ● The biblical backdrop is twofold. **(1)** The collapse of Jericho, an event that gave Israel a decisive hold on the Promised Land, likewise followed seven trumpet blasts (Josh 6:1–21). **(2)** The declaration in 11:15 recalls the dream of Nebuchadnezzer (Dan 2:31–36), in which the eternal kingdom of God destroys the godless kingdoms of the world (Dan 2:44–45). See note on Rev 10:7.

11:17 who are and who were: A shortened form of the title in 1:4, 8 and 4:8. The omission of the future element "who is to come" here and in 16:5 is deliberate, signaling that God has at last come as King and Judge over the earth (11:15). The manifestation of God's kingdom may be linked with the trampling down of Jerusalem, as in Lk 21:31 (cf. Zech 14:1–9).

11:19 ark of his covenant: The throne of God in the heavenly temple. From its base issue divine judgments symbolized by violent thunderstorms and earthquakes (4:5; 16:17–18). ● John sees the heavenly counterpart to the ancient ark where Yahweh sat invisibly enthroned in the sanctuaries of Israel (2 Sam 6:2; Is 37:16).

12:1—14:20 A narrative interlude between the judgment of the seven trumpets (8:6—11:19) and the judgment of the seven bowls (15:1—16:21). This central section may be seen as developing around seven spiritual figures (woman, 12:1; dragon, 12:3; male child, 12:5; Michael, 12:7; sea beast, 13:1; land beast, 13:11; the Lamb, 14:1).

12:1–6 The **woman** of Revelation 12 is both an individual person and a collective symbol. She is Mary, the Mother of the Messiah and the spiritual mother of his disciples (Jn 19:26–27). But she also represents the faithful of Israel, crying out for the Messiah (Rev 12:2), as well as the Church, attacked by the devil for witnessing to Jesus (12:17) (CCC 501, 507, 1138). ● The depiction of the woman is rich in biblical symbolism. **(1)** Antagonism between the woman and the **dragon**, the "ancient serpent" (12:9), recalls Gen 3:15, the first prophecy in Scripture to foretell the demise of the devil through the offspring (Messiah) of a woman (a new Eve). **(2)** Images of the **sun**, **moon**, and **stars** call to mind Gen 37:9–10, where they symbolize the family of Israel, namely, Jacob, his wife, and his twelve sons. **(3)** The **pangs** and **anguish** of childbirth recall Isaiah's description of Daughter Zion, a maternal figure that represents the holy remnant of Israel groaning for redemption (Is 26:17; Mic 4:9–10). **(4)** Because the woman is a queen who wears a **crown** and a mother who bears a royal

---

[d] Greek *spiritually.*

50

pangs of birth, in anguish for delivery. ³And another sign appeared in heaven; behold, a great red dragon, with seven heads and ten horns, and seven diadems upon his heads. ⁴His tail swept down a third of the stars of heaven, and cast them to the earth. And the dragon stood before the woman who was about to bear a child, that he might devour her child when she brought it forth; ⁵she brought forth a male child, one who is to rule all the nations with a rod of iron, but her child was caught up to God and to his throne, ⁶and the woman fled into the wilderness, where she has a place prepared by God, in which to be nourished for one thousand two hundred and sixty days.

Michael Defeats the Dragon

7 Now war arose in heaven, Michael and his angels fighting against the dragon; and the dragon and his angels fought, ⁸but they were defeated and there was no longer any place for them in heaven. ⁹And the great dragon was thrown down, that ancient serpent, who is called the Devil and Satan, the deceiver of the whole world—he was thrown down to the earth, and his angels were thrown down with him. ¹⁰And I heard a loud voice in heaven, saying, "Now the salvation and the power and the kingdom of our God and the authority of his Christ have come, for the accuser of our brethren has been thrown down, who accuses them day and night before our God. ¹¹And they have conquered him by the blood of the Lamb and by the word of their testimony, for they loved not their lives even unto death. ¹²Rejoice then, O heaven and you that dwell therein! But woe to you, O earth and sea, for the devil has come down to you in great wrath, because he knows that his time is short!"

The Dragon Makes War against the Woman's Offspring

13 And when the dragon saw that he had been thrown down to the earth, he pursued the woman who had borne the male child. ¹⁴But the woman was given the two wings of the great eagle that she might fly from the serpent into the wilderness, to the place where she is to be nourished for a time, and times, and half a time. ¹⁵The serpent poured water like a river out of his mouth after the woman, to sweep her away with the flood. ¹⁶But the earth came to the help of the woman, and the

---

12:3: Dan 7:7.   **12:4:** Dan 8:10.   **12:5:** Is 66:7; Ps 2:9.   **12:7:** Dan 10:13.   **12:9:** Gen 3:1, 14–15; Zech 3:1.
12:10: Job 1:9–11.   **12:12:** Is 44:23; 49:13.   **12:14:** Dan 7:25; 12:7.

---

male child, she is also the Queen Mother of the Davidic kingdom reestablished by Jesus, the Davidic male child (1 Kings 2:19-20; Jer 13:18) (CCC 489). See essay: *Queen Mother* at 1 Kings 2. ● The woman is clearly the Church, endowed with the Word of the Father, whose brightness outshines the sun. Like the moon she is adorned with heavenly glory, and her crown of twelve stars points to the twelve apostles who founded the Church (St. Hippolytus, *On the Antichrist* 61). The vision speaks of the Mother of our Savior, depicting her in heaven, not on earth, as pure in body and soul, as equal to an angel, as one of heaven's citizens, as one who brought about the Incarnation of God. She has nothing in common with this world and its evils but is exalted and worthy of heaven, despite her descent from our mortal nature (Oecumenius, *Commentary on the Apocalypse* 6, 19).

12:1 the moon: Can symbolize both maternal dignity (Gen 37:9-10) and feminine beauty (Song 6:10). **twelve stars:** Represent both the twelve tribes of Israel (21:12) and the twelve apostles of Jesus (21:14).

12:2 pangs of birth: This is probably related to the Passion of Jesus, which pierced the heart of his Mother (Lk 2:35) and seized his disciples with the distress of a woman in labor (Jn 16:20-22).

12:3 red dragon: Represents Satan, the murderous arch enemy of God (Jn 8:44). His **horns** are symbols of his strength (Dan 7:7), and his **diadems** (crowns) are symbols of his ruling power over the fallen world (Jn 12:31). He is doomed to burn forever in the lake of fire (Rev 20:10). ● The draconic serpent was a mythological symbol of evil in the ancient Near East. Called Leviathan (Is 27:1) or Rahab (Job 26:12-13), he was pictured as a sea monster with multiple heads (Ps 74:14).

12:4 a third of the stars: A flashback to the fall of the angels at the dawn of creation (2 Pet 2:4). The imagery hints at how Satan led the rebellion, dragging a host of demons down with him (CCC 391-92). In the Bible, stars often represent angels (Rev 1:20; 9:1; Judg 5:20; Job 38:7).

12:5 male child: His coming forth symbolizes both the birth and rebirth (Resurrection) of Jesus as the Davidic Messiah. ● The **rod of iron** alludes to Ps 2:9, a coronation psalm that celebrates the enthronement and royal adoption (i.e., divine birth) of the Davidic kings of Israel. It is ultimately fulfilled in Christ, who rose to an immortal life of kingship (Acts 13:33) when he ascended into glory (Heb 1:5-8). **caught up to God:** Refers to the Ascension, which culminated the heavenly enthronement of Christ next to the Father (3:21; Mk 16:19).

12:6 fled into the wilderness: Many interpret this as the safe escape of Jewish Christians from Jerusalem when they fled to a place called Pella. See note on Rev 11:2.

12:7 Michael: The heavenly warrior and archangel (Jude 9) who protects the People of God (Dan 12:1). Here he leads the heavenly army in the attack against Satan and his hoards.

12:9 that ancient serpent: Satan, who took the form of a reptile when he instigated the fall of man in Gen 3:1-13. His name in Greek is the **Devil**, meaning "slanderer", and his name in Hebrew is **Satan**, meaning "adversary". **the deceiver:** Satan is the father of every lie and falsehood (Jn 8:44).

12:10 Now the salvation: Heaven celebrates the expulsion of the devil and his angels. This is not the fall of the angels at the dawn of time (12:4), but the defeat of evil at the turning point of salvation history, when Christ mounted the Cross and cast out the ruler of this world (Jn 12:31-32; Col 2:15). **the kingdom:** See note on Rev 11:15-19. **accuser of our brethren:** The devil is a prosecuting attorney who makes damning accusations against the saints (Job 1:6-11; Zech 3:1).

12:11 conquered . . . unto death: The martyrs appear defeated by death but are actually victorious. They, most of all, have shown the greater love (Jn 15:13) that makes them like Christ, even in his death (Phil 3:10).

12:13-17 Slammed down to earth, the devil storms off after the woman, but God protects her from his evil intentions. ● The imagery recalls how Yahweh was said to have rescued Israel from Egypt on eagle's **wings** (12:14; Ex 19:4). Other allusions include the salvation of Noah's family from the **flood** (12:15; Gen 6-8) and the destruction of Korah and his rebel supporters when the earth **opened its mouth** to swallow them alive (12:16; Num 16:1-34).

earth opened its mouth and swallowed the river which the dragon had poured from his mouth. [17]Then the dragon was angry with the woman, and went off to make war on the rest of her offspring, on those who keep the commandments of God and bear testimony to Jesus. And he stood[e] on the sand of the sea.

The Beast from the Sea

13 And I saw a beast rising out of the sea, with ten horns and seven heads, with ten diadems upon its horns and a blasphemous name upon its heads. [2]And the beast that I saw was like a leopard, its feet were like a bear's, and its mouth was like a lion's mouth. And to it the dragon gave his power and his throne and great authority. [3]One of its heads seemed to have a mortal wound, but its mortal wound was healed, and the whole earth followed the beast with wonder. [4]Men worshiped the dragon, for he had given his authority to the beast, and they worshiped the beast, saying, "Who is like the beast, and who can fight against it?"

5 And the beast was given a mouth uttering haughty and blasphemous words, and it was al-lowed to exercise authority for forty-two months; [6]it opened its mouth to utter blasphemies against God, blaspheming his name and his dwelling, that is, those who dwell in heaven. [7]Also it was allowed to make war on the saints and to conquer them.[f] And authority was given it over every tribe and people and tongue and nation, [8]and all who dwell on earth will worship it, every one whose name has not been written before the foundation of the world in the book of life of the Lamb that was slain. [9]If any one has an ear, let him hear:
[10]If any one is to be taken captive,
   to captivity he goes;
if any one slays with the sword,
   with the sword must he be slain.
Here is a call for the endurance and faith of the saints.

The Beast from the Earth

11 Then I saw another beast which rose out of the earth; it had two horns like a lamb and it spoke like a dragon. [12]It exercises all the authority of the first beast in its presence, and makes the earth and its inhabitants worship the first beast, whose

---

13:1: Dan 7:1–6.   **13:5:** Dan 7:8.   **13:7:** Dan 7:21.
13:9: Mk 4:23.   **13:10:** Jer 15:2.

12:17 the woman . . . her offspring: An allusion to Gen 3:15, which stands as a backdrop for the entire chapter. Here the woman's offspring is not only the Messiah (individual, 12:5), but also his disciples (collective, Rom 16:20). See note on Rev 12:1–6.

13:1–18 Chapter 13 introduces two agents of the dragon: one is a beast from the **sea** (13:1), and another is a beast from the **earth** (13:11). The sea beast is surely the Roman Empire, while the land beast seems to represent a corrupt religious authority. See note on Rev 13:11.

13:1–2 a beast rising out of the sea: Several parallels indicate that the sea beast, as a demonic rival, mimics the Lamb. **(1)** The Lamb is worshiped by angels and saints (5:14), while the beast is worshiped by the wicked (13:4); **(2)** the Lamb was slain and rose again (5:6), while the beast was mortally wounded and recovered (13:3); **(3)** the Lamb sits on the throne of his Father (3:21), while the beast shares a throne with the dragon (13:2); **(4)** the Lamb redeems believers from every tribe and nation (5:9), while the beast has temporal authority over every tribe and nation (13:7); **(5)** the Lamb is worthy of power and glory from God (5:12), while the beast receives power and authority from the dragon (13:2); **(6)** the name of the Lamb is stamped on the foreheads of the saints (14:1), while the number of the beast is branded on brows of sinners (13:16-18). ● The imagery comes from Dan 7:1-7, where the pagan empires that oppressed Israel in exilic and postexilic times appear as four beasts rising up out of the sea—a lion, a bear, a leopard, and a creature with ten horns. Their animal features are here combined into an image of imperial Rome, who embodies the power and ferocity of them all.

13:3 One of its heads: The seven heads of the beast represent seven Roman kings, according to 17:9-10. **mortal wound . . . healed:** The wounded head is probably Caesar Nero, who committed suicide in June A.D. 68. He was the last of Julius Caesar's dynastic line, and his death threw Rome into political chaos and civil war. Though many thought the Empire had ended with the demise of Nero, a new claimant gained control of the throne (Galba), and the Empire lived on. Others read this as an allusion to the Nero *redivivus* legend, an ancient belief the Nero would someday return and reclaim his authority as Roman dictator. See notes on Rev 13:18 and 17:10.

13:5 forty-two months: A time of limited but intense tribulation. See note on Rev 11:2.

13:6 his dwelling: The heavenly sanctuary inhabited by the saints (7:15).

13:7 war on the saints: Believers become martyrs when they refuse to worship the beast and its image (13:15; 20:4). According to some, this alludes to the Neronian persecution of the Church in the mid 60s; for others, the Domitian persecution of the late first century is in view (CCC 2113). ● The passage recalls the violence of the fourth beast in Dan 7:21.

13:8 the book of life: A heavenly registry of the saints. See note on Rev 20:12.

13:10 If any one: An allusion to Jer 15:2 and 43:11, where Jeremiah learns that tragedy was certain to befall the sinners of Judah and Jerusalem, for Yahweh had decreed their captivity and death. In this context, the oracle is an exhortation to endurance, either assuring believers that God will bring judgment on their persecutors or calling them to remain faithful in spite of imprisonment (captivity) and martyrdom (sword). **slays with the sword:** Another manuscript reading has this in the passive voice: "is to be slain with the sword".

13:11 another beast: A land beast as distinct from the sea beast of 13:1. Because its power is used to promote false worship (13:12), most think that it represents a religious entity subordinate to the secular State embodied in the first beast. It is identified differently by different scholars. **(1)** Those who date Revelation in the 60s tend to identify this beast with the religious leadership of Israel centered in Jerusalem. This is the priestly and juridical body that rejected the kingship of Christ and pledged its allegiance to Caesar (Jn 19:15). Thereafter it was primarily Jewish leaders who aroused opposition against the early Christians and accused them before Roman authorities (Rev 2:9; 3:9; Acts 14:2; 17:5-7; 18:12-13; 24:9; 25:1-7, 24). Also, the land beast is later called a "false prophet" (Rev 16:13; 19:20; 20:10). This may be significant in light of Jesus' warning that false prophets would arise to deceive and perform

---

[e] Other ancient authorities read *And I stood*, connecting the sentence with 13:1.
[f] Other ancient authorities omit this sentence.

mortal wound was healed. [13]It works great signs, even making fire come down from heaven to earth in the sight of men; [14]and by the signs which it is allowed to work in the presence of the beast, it deceives those who dwell on earth, bidding them make an image for the beast which was wounded by the sword and yet lived; [15]and it was allowed to give breath to the image of the beast so that the image of the beast should even speak, and to cause those who would not worship the image of the beast to be slain. [16]Also it causes all, both small and great, both rich and poor, both free and slave, to be marked on the right hand or the forehead, [17]so that no one can buy or sell unless he has the mark, that is, the name of the beast or the number of its name. [18]This calls for wisdom: let him who has understanding reckon the number of the beast, for it is a human number, its number is six hundred and sixty-six. [g]

The Lamb and the 144,000

14 Then I looked, and behold, on Mount Zion stood the Lamb, and with him a hundred and forty-four thousand who had his name and his Father's name written on their foreheads. [2]And I heard a voice from heaven like the sound of many waters and like the sound of loud thunder; the voice I heard was like the sound of harpists playing on their harps, [3]and they sing a new song before the throne and before the four living creatures and before the elders. No one could learn that song except the hundred and forty-four thousand who had been redeemed from the earth. [4]It is these who have not defiled themselves with women, for they are chaste; [h] it is these who follow the Lamb wherever he goes; these have been redeemed from mankind as first fruits for God and the Lamb, [5]and in their mouth no lie was found, for they are spotless.

The Messages of the Three Angels

6 Then I saw another angel flying in midheaven, with an eternal gospel to proclaim to those who dwell on earth, to every nation and tribe and tongue and people; [7]and he said with a loud voice, "Fear God and give him glory, for the hour of his

---

13:14: Deut 13:1–5.   **13:15:** Dan 3:5.   **14:1:** Ezek 9:4.

---

signs in the days before Jerusalem's doom (compare Rev 13:13–14 with Mt 24:11, 24). **(2)** Those who date the book in the 90s identify the land beast with the custodians of Roman civil religion, specifically, the cult of the emperors. Its basis was the deification of the Roman Caesars, to whom temples were dedicated and whose images were placed throughout the Empire. Loyalty to the divine ruler was expressed by worship, with each citizen making a small offering of wine and incense before the ruler's statue. Refusal to participate was not only frowned upon but was gradually regarded as a punishable crime. History shows that Christians were faced with this option of religious apostasy or Roman punishment from at least the second century A.D. (Pliny the Younger, *Epistles* 10, 96).

13:13 great signs: The land beast is empowered to dazzle the wicked with displays of its power (cf. 2 Thess 2:9–10). **fire . . . from heaven:** A demonic replication of the miracles of Elijah (1 Kings 18:38; 2 Kings 1:10–14).

13:14 an image: An idol to be worshiped. ● Allusion is made to Dan 3:1–7, where King Nebuchadnezzar of Babylon erected a colossal image and decreed that all must bow in worship before the idol under pain of death. The pious Shadrach, Meshach, and Abednego became protomartyrs when they refused and were cast into the fiery furnace (Dan 3:8–23).

13:17 the mark: A sign of apostasy. By demanding the mark, the beast forces believers to choose between prosperity and poverty, material wealth and martyrdom. It is uncertain what historical circumstances underlie this description. However, standard coinage minted in Tyre and used throughout Syria-Palestine was discontinued in the late 50s, eventually passing out of circulation. In its place, new coins were minted in Antioch with an image of Emperor Nero (see note on Rev 13:18). This may in part explain "buying and selling" in connection with "the beast", especially since the Greek term for "mark" can refer to an image struck on a coin.

13:18 six hundred and sixty-six: A number directly linked with the "name" of the beast (13:17). It is probably a cryptogram for Nero Caesar, whose name written in Hebrew adds up to 666. Interestingly, when the Greek word for "beast" is written in Hebrew letters, it too adds up to 666. A few ancient manuscripts list the number as 616, which is the value of Nero's name according to its Latin spelling. In any case, describing Nero as the beast is entirely apt: he was a man of exceeding cruelty and moral depravity and was the first emperor to order a bloody persecution of Christians (Tacitus, *Annals* 15, 44). See notes on Rev 13:3 and 17:10. ● The numeral 666 appears in the Bible only here and in connection with Solomon, who received 666 talents of gold in a single year (1 Kings 10:14; 2 Chron 9:13). This was the beginning of Solomon's end, for his wealth turned him away from the Lord. Solomon typifies the beast to the extent that he allowed material prosperity to corrupt the People of God.

14:1 Mount Zion: The heavenly summit crowned with the heavenly Jerusalem (21:2). The earthly Zion, where the historical city of Jerusalem was first made an Israelite settlement (2 Sam 5:7), is a visible model of this celestial height (Gal 4:26; Heb 12:22). ● Zion looms large in the OT as the focal point of Israel's brightest hopes for the future. It is the glorified city and mountain where the redeemed will be gathered to the Lord (Is 4:2–6; Joel 3:17; Obad 21; Mic 4:1–7). John's vision of a remnant without a "lie" in their mouths (Rev 14:5) connects directly with this tradition (Zeph 3:11–13). **hundred and forty-four thousand:** The faithful of Israel sealed on their foreheads. See note on Rev 7:4. **his name . . . Father's name:** In contrast to the numerical name of the beast branded on the foreheads of the wicked (13:16–17) (CCC 2159).

14:2 harps: Traditional accompaniment for liturgical song (Ps 33:2).

14:3 a new song: A song of praise that celebrates the salvation of God. See note on Rev 5:9.

14:4 they are chaste: Literally, "they are virgins." This probably has two levels of meaning. **(1)** The assembly is made up of celibate men whose *bodies* have never been given to women. **(2)** The assembly is made up of holy men whose *souls* have not been defiled by the impurities of the harlot city (17:1–6; 18:3) (CCC 1618–19). ● "The Lamb walks the way of virginity. Follow him there, you virgins, for on this count you follow him wherever he goes. . . . The masses of the faithful, unable to follow the Lamb to this blessing, will rejoice with you; but they will not be able to sing that new song which is for you alone" (St. Augustine, *On Holy Virginity* 29).

14:6 another angel flying in midheaven: Seven angels have already been described in chaps. 8–10. The first flying in midheaven appears in 8:13 as an eagle. **eternal gospel:** The

---

[g] Other ancient authorities read *six hundred and sixteen*.
[h] Greek *virgins*.

judgment has come; and worship him who made heaven and earth, the sea and the fountains of water."

8 Another angel, a second, followed, saying, "Fallen, fallen is Babylon the great, she who made all nations drink the wine of her impure passion."

9 And another angel, a third, followed them, saying with a loud voice, "If any one worships the beast and its image, and receives a mark on his forehead or on his hand, [10]he also shall drink the wine of God's wrath, poured unmixed into the cup of his anger, and he shall be tormented with fire and brimstone in the presence of the holy angels and in the presence of the Lamb. [11]And the smoke of their torment goes up for ever and ever; and they have no rest, day or night, these worshipers of the beast and its image, and whoever receives the mark of its name."

12 Here is a call for the endurance of the saints, those who keep the commandments of God and the faith of Jesus.

13 And I heard a voice from heaven saying, "Write this: Blessed are the dead who from now on die in the Lord." "Blessed indeed," says the Spirit, "that they may rest from their labors, for their deeds follow them!"

Reaping the Earth's Harvest

14 Then I looked, and behold, a white cloud, and seated on the cloud one like a son of man, with a golden crown on his head, and a sharp sickle in his hand. [15]And another angel came out of the temple, calling with a loud voice to him who sat upon the cloud, "Put in your sickle, and reap, for the hour to reap has come, for the harvest of the earth is fully ripe." [16]So he who sat upon the cloud swung his sickle on the earth, and the earth was reaped.

17 And another angel came out of the temple in heaven, and he too had a sharp sickle. [18]Then another angel came out from the altar, the angel who has power over fire, and he called with a loud voice to him who had the sharp sickle, "Put in your sickle, and gather the clusters of the vine of the earth, for its grapes are ripe." [19]So the angel swung his sickle on the earth and gathered the vintage of the earth, and threw it into the great wine press of the wrath of God; [20]and the wine press was trodden outside the city, and blood flowed from the wine press, as high as a horse's bridle, for one thousand six hundred stadia. [1]

The Angels with the Seven Last Plagues

15 Then I saw another sign in heaven, great and wonderful, seven angels with seven plagues, which are the last, for with them the wrath of God is ended.

2 And I saw what appeared to be a sea of glass mingled with fire, and those who had conquered the beast and its image and the number of its name,

---

14:8: Is 21:9.   **14:10:** Jer 51:7; Gen 19:24.   **14:11:** Is 34:10.   **14:14:** Dan 7:13.
14:15: Joel 3:13; Mt 13:30.   **14:20:** Joel 3:13.   **15:1:** Lev 26:21.

---

invitation to fear and worship the one true God, the Creator of all (14:7). It is a call for the followers of the beast to abandon their idols before judgment falls (14:18).

📖 **14:8 Babylon:** The ancient city and superpower of Mesopotamia built along the Euphrates River (modern Iraq). It was infamous for its moral decadence and is remembered in Scripture as the blasphemous power that destroyed Jerusalem in the sixth century B.C. See essay: *Who is Babylon?* at Rev 18. ● Proclamation that Babylon has fallen draws from Is 21:9 and Jer 51:7–8 and anticipates the vision in Rev 18:1–24. As in these oracles, the angel speaks of something about to happen (prophecy) as if it were already accomplished (past history).

📖 **14:10 cup of his anger:** The wicked will be forced to drink God's wrath like bitter wine from a cup (Ps 75:8; Is 51:17; Jer 25:15). **fire and brimstone:** An advance glimpse of the lake of fire and sulfur that burns eternally (20:10). ● The damnation of the godless evokes memories of the fiery destruction of Sodom and Gomorrah (Gen 19:24; Ps 11:6).

14:11 they have no rest: In contrast to the righteous, who die in Christ (14:13).

14:13 Blessed are the dead: The second of seven beatitudes in Revelation. See note on Rev 1:3.

📖 **14:14–20** The judgment of the righteous and the wicked is described in terms of a great harvest. The saints are gathered up like sheaves of wheat to be stored in a granary (14:16; Jn 4:35–38), while sinners are severed like grapes from the vine to be thrown into a mill press and crushed (14:19). ● Similar scenes of divine judgment appear in the prophets (Is 63:1–6; Jer 51:33; Lam 1:15; Joel 3:13).

14:14 son of man: Jesus Christ, described as the royal figure from Dan 7:13. See note on Rev 1:7 and essay: *Jesus, the Son of Man* at Lk 17.

14:19 wine press: A stone trough used to trample or otherwise squeeze the juice from grapes.

14:20 the city: Called "Babylon" (14:8). **one thousand six hundred stadia:** About 185 miles. Some take this to mean that divine judgment will extend over the land of Israel, which is roughly this distance measured north to south. Others read the number as symbolic of completeness (40 × 40 stadia) and envision a worldwide judgment. Either way, the horrific quantity of blood indicates the severity of God's wrath on those who defy him.

15:1—16:21 The final cycle of judgments in Revelation are the seven bowls of wrath, which douse the earth with plagues poured down from heaven. Though parallels can be traced between the seven bowls and the seven trumpets (8:6—11:19), the bowl judgments are more devastating and extensive.

15:1 another sign: Following the sign of the woman and the dragon in 12:1–3.

📖✝ **15:2–4** John sees and hears the martyrs of heaven standing beside the glassy sea and singing praises to God. ● They sing an adaptation of the **song of Moses** from Ex 15:1–18. This was the victory song chanted by the Israelites as they celebrated their deliverance from Egypt on the shores of the Red Sea. Here the saints celebrate a new Exodus from the sin and slavery of the world. For the Exodus theme, see note on Rev 5:9–10. ● The entire Exodus from Egypt was a type of the Church's coming forth from the Gentiles. In the end, the Lord will lead her out of this world into his own inheritance, which was not conferred by Moses, the servant of God, but by Jesus, the Son of God (St. Irenaeus, *Against Heresies* 4, 30, 4).

15:2 sea of glass: See note on Rev 4:5–6. **conquered:** The

---

[1] About two hundred miles.

standing beside the sea of glass with harps of God in their hands. [3]And they sing the song of Moses, the servant of God, and the song of the Lamb, saying,

"Great and wonderful are your deeds,
O Lord God the Almighty!
Just and true are your ways,
O King of the ages! [j]
[4]Who shall not fear and glorify your name, O
  Lord?
For you alone are holy.
All nations shall come and worship you,
for your judgments have been revealed."

5 After this I looked, and the temple of the tent of witness in heaven was opened, [6]and out of the temple came the seven angels with the seven plagues, robed in pure bright linen, and with golden sashes across their chests. [7]And one of the four living creatures gave the seven angels seven golden bowls full of the wrath of God who lives for ever and ever; [8]and the temple was filled with smoke from the glory of God and from his power, and no one could enter the temple until the seven plagues of the seven angels were ended.

The Bowls of God's Wrath

16 Then I heard a loud voice from the temple telling the seven angels, "Go and pour out on the earth the seven bowls of the wrath of God."

2 So the first angel went and poured his bowl on the earth, and foul and evil sores came upon the men who bore the mark of the beast and worshiped its image.

3 The second angel poured his bowl into the sea, and it became like the blood of a dead man, and every living thing died that was in the sea.

4 The third angel poured his bowl into the rivers and the fountains of water, and they became blood. [5]And I heard the angel of water say,

"Just are you in these your judgments,
  you who are and were, O Holy One.
[6]For men have shed the blood of saints and
  prophets,
  and you have given them blood to drink.
It is their due!"
[7]And I heard the altar cry,
"Yes, Lord God the Almighty,
  true and just are your judgments!"

8 The fourth angel poured his bowl on the sun, and it was allowed to scorch men with fire; [9]men were scorched by the fierce heat, and they cursed the name of God who had power over these plagues, and they did not repent and give him glory.

10 The fifth angel poured his bowl on the throne of the beast, and its kingdom was in darkness; men gnawed their tongues in anguish [11]and cursed the God of heaven for their pain and sores, and did not repent of their deeds.

12 The sixth angel poured his bowl on the great river Euphra´tes, and its water was dried up,

---

15:3: Ex 15:1; Ps 145:17.   **15:4:** Jer 10:7; Ps 86:9–10.   **15:5:** Ex 40:34.   **15:8:** 1 Kings 8:10; Is 6:4; Ezek 44:4.
16:1: Is 66:6; Ps 69:24.   **16:2:** Ex 9:10–11; Deut 28:35.   **16:3–4:** Ex 7:17–21.   **16:6:** Ps 79:3.   **16:7:** Ps 119:137.
16:10: Ex 10:21.   **16:12:** Is 11:15–16.

---

martyrs attacked by the dragon and the sea beast reign victorious through the blood of the Lamb (12:11; 13:7).

15:3 Just and true are your ways: Probably an allusion to the Greek version of Deut 32:4, which is part of another OT canticle called the Song of Moses (Deut 32:1–43).

15:5 the temple: Perhaps the inner chamber of the **tent of witness**, which is the heavenly counterpart to the earthly Tabernacle erected by Moses (Heb 8:1–5). For the liturgical imagery and setting of John's visions, see note on Rev 4:1—5:14.

15:6 bright linen: Priestly garments (Lev 16:4) that symbolize purity and righteousness (19:8). **golden sashes:** Another article of priestly attire. Jesus wears a golden sash as the heavenly high priest in 1:13.

15:7 seven golden bowls: Liturgical bowls like the ones used to carry incense in 5:8. The use of holy vessels to pour out the plagues reinforces the idea that God's judgments are holy and just (15:4).

15:8 filled with smoke: Entrance into the heavenly throne room is cut off by the glorious cloud of God's presence. ● This recalls how the fiery cloud of the Lord filled the Mosaic Tabernacle (Ex 40:34–35) and the Solomonic Temple (1 Kings 8:10–11), making entrance temporarily impossible. Isaiah experienced this firsthand when he saw the Lord enthroned in the Temple (Is 6:1–4).

16:1–21 One by one, the seven angels are summoned to dump the seven bowls of wrath upon the world. Unlike the sequence of seven seals and seven trumpets, where an interlude separated the sixth and seventh calamity, the seven bowls are poured in direct succession, without an intermission above or relief for those below. ● Several of the seven bowls are modeled on the Exodus plagues that ravaged Egypt. This can be seen in the **sores** (16:2, sixth plague, Ex 9:8–12), the water sources turned into **blood** (16:3–4, first plague, Ex 7:17–21), the **darkness** (16:10, ninth plague, Ex 10:21–23), the demonic **frogs** (16:13, second plague, Ex 8:2–6), and the heavy **hail** (16:21, seventh plague, Ex 9:18–35). For similar connections with the trumpets, see note on Rev 8:7—11:19.

16:5 you who are and were: Part of the threefold title of God in 1:4, here without the future element: "who is to come". For the significance of this, see note on Rev 11:17.

16:6 saints and prophets: Martyred in the "great city" destined to be destroyed (18:24).

16:7 the altar cry: The pleas of the martyrs are at last answered as God avenges their blood on those who killed them (6:9–11).

16:9 men were scorched: The wicked are seared by the sun, while the righteous are protected in the shade of God's presence (7:16). **did not repent:** Even the crushing weight of divine curses did not bring the wicked to their knees and induce them to mend their ways (16:11).

16:10 throne of the beast: The throne of the dragon, which he shares with the beast from the sea (13:2). Historically, the darkness that ensues may be linked with the death of Nero, whose suicide in June A.D. 68 sparked considerable upheaval in the Empire. See note on Rev 13:3.

16:12 river Euphrates: Runs through Mesopotamia, to the **east** of Israel beyond the northern Arabian desert. The Babylonian army had to cross this river when it advanced toward Jerusalem to destroy it in the sixth century B.C.

---

[j] Other ancient authorities read *the nations*.

to prepare the way for the kings from the east. [13]And I saw, issuing from the mouth of the dragon and from the mouth of the beast and from the mouth of the false prophet, three foul spirits like frogs; [14]for they are demonic spirits, performing signs, who go abroad to the kings of the whole world, to assemble them for battle on the great day of God the Almighty. [15]("Behold, I am coming like a thief! Blessed is he who is awake, keeping his garments that he may not go naked and be seen exposed!") [16]And they assembled them at the place which is called in Hebrew Armaged′don.

17 The seventh angel poured his bowl into the air, and a great voice came out of the temple, from the throne, saying, "It is done!" [18]And there were flashes of lightning, loud noises, peals of thunder, and a great earthquake such as had never been since men were on the earth, so great was that earthquake. [19]The great city was split into three parts, and the cities of the nations fell, and God remembered great Babylon, to make her drain the cup of the fury of his wrath. [20]And every island fled away, and no mountains were to be found; [21]and great hailstones, heavy as a hundredweight, dropped on men from heaven, till men cursed God for the plague of the hail, so fearful was that plague.

The Great Whore and the Beast

17 Then one of the seven angels who had the seven bowls came and said to me, "Come, I will show you the judgment of the great harlot who is seated upon many waters, [2]with whom the kings of the earth have committed fornication, and with the wine of whose fornication the dwellers on earth have become drunk." [3]And he carried me away in the Spirit into a wilderness, and I saw a woman sitting on a scarlet beast which was full of blasphemous names, and it had seven heads and ten horns. [4]The woman was clothed in purple and scarlet, and adorned with gold and jewels and pearls, holding in her hand a golden cup full of abominations and the impurities of her fornication; [5]and on her forehead was written a name of mystery: "Babylon the great, mother of harlots and of earth's abominations." [6]And I saw the woman, drunk with the blood of the saints and the blood of the martyrs of Jesus.

When I saw her I marveled greatly. [7]But the angel said to me, "Why marvel? I will tell you the mystery of the woman, and of the beast with seven

---

16:13: 1 Kings 22:21–23; Ex 8:3.   **16:15:** 1 Thess 5:2.   **16:16:** 2 Kings 9:27.   **16:17:** Is 66:6.   **16:18:** Ex 19:16; Dan 12:1.   **16:21:** Ex 9:23.   **17:1:** Jer 51:13.   **17:2:** Is 23:17; Jer 25:15–16.   **17:4:** Jer 51:7.

16:13 the false prophet: The land beast of 13:11.

16:15 Blessed is he: The third of seven beatitudes in Revelation. See note on Rev 1:3.

16:16 Armageddon: Means "mountain of Megiddo" in Hebrew. Megiddo was a fortified settlement in central Israel overlooking a broad plain that was used as a battlefield in biblical times. Revelation envisions another conflict staged near Megiddo, one destined to end with the devastation of the harlot city (chaps. 17–18) along with the defeat of the beast and the false prophet (19:11–21). Ultimately, this catastrophic event serves as a preview of the final battle between good and evil scheduled for the end of time (20:7–10). ● The plain of Megiddo evokes memories of victory and defeat. Here Israel routed the Canaanites and secured several decades of peace in the time of the Judges (Judg 5:19–21). Here, too, King Josiah of Judah stubbornly refused to stay out of a foreign skirmish and, as a result, fell on the battlefield and caused great mourning in Israel (2 Chron 35:20–25; Zech 12:11).

16:17–21 The seventh bowl brings the final crushing blow upon wicked Babylon. Forced to swallow every last drop of God's **wrath** (16:19), it is at last shaken apart by an **earthquake** (16:18) and pounded to the ground with huge **hailstones** (16:21).

17:1—18:24 The visions that follow are directly related to the seventh bowl of wrath in 16:17–21, giving a more in-depth look at this final calamity.

17:1–6 John sees a seductive **harlot** riding atop a **scarlet beast**. The woman, popularly known as the whore of Babylon, is said to be "the great city" (17:18), a title earlier given to the city where Jesus was crucified (11:8). The beast, having seven heads and ten horns, was earlier described as the beast from the sea (13:1) and appears to be the Roman Empire, with its capital city Rome represented by seven hills (17:9). For background, see notes on Rev 11:8, 13:1–2, and essay: *Who Is Babylon?* at Rev 18. ● Sinful cities are sometimes described as harlots in the Bible. On two occasions, this is said of a pagan metropolis, one being Tyre (Is 23:17) and the other Nineveh (Nahum 3:4). However, the charge is proverbially made against Jerusalem for her spiritual promiscuity with pagan nations (Is 1:21; Jer 2:20; Ezek 16:1–25; 23:1–4, 11, 30).

17:1 seated: Symbolizes the unholy alliance between the harlot city and the pagan power with whom she is united in opposition to the Christian message. Multiple images are used to depict these partners in crime but always with the same posture: John sees a harlot *seated* on the waters (17:1, 15), a woman *sitting* on a beast (17:3), and a woman *seated* on seven hills (17:9). Violent action was taken against early Christians by both the harlot city (17:6; 18:24) and the beast (11:7; 13:7). **many waters:** Symbolic of the Gentile world, according to 17:15. It fittingly stands for the multinational Roman Empire. ● Allusion is made to the Greek version of Jer 51:13, which depicts ancient Babylon dwelling upon "many waters".

17:2 fornication: The language of sexual immorality is symbolic of spiritual immorality. In the Bible, acts of harlotry point to transgressions of the covenant, such as idolatry and alliances with godless nations (cf. Ex 34:15–16; Ezek 16:26–29; 23:30; Hos 1:2). **wine:** Sins of violence have filled the harlot's cup with the innocent blood of Christians (17:6).

17:3 in the Spirit: The Greek expression, which also appears in 1:10 and 21:10, is ambiguous. As rendered in the RSV, it suggests John's visions are granted by the Holy Spirit and consist of mystical experiences perceived to be in different locations. It could also be translated "in spirit" and refer to John's interior awareness of the revelations he received. **scarlet beast:** Resembles the Satanic dragon in color (red, 12:3) and appearance (seven heads and ten horns, 12:3).

17:4 scarlet . . . gold: Jeremiah once described Judah and Jerusalem as a harlot (Jer 2:20) dressed in scarlet and decked in gold finery (Jer 4:30). Ezekiel likewise pictured Jerusalem as a young woman arrayed in gold and fine linen (Ezek 16:13) who became a harlot (Ezek 16:2, 15). **golden cup:** The image comes from Jer 51:7, which depicts Babylon as a golden cup filled with the wine of madness.

17:5 her forehead: Recalls the mark of the beast (13:16–18).

17:6 drunk with the blood: I.e., guilty of murderous bloodshed (18:24). ● The vision recalls OT laws that declare the consumption of blood an abomination before the Lord (Lev 3:17; 17:10).

heads and ten horns that carries her. ⁸The beast that you saw was, and is not, and is to ascend from the bottomless pit and go to perdition; and the dwellers on earth whose names have not been written in the book of life from the foundation of the world, will marvel to behold the beast, because it was and is not and is to come. ⁹This calls for a mind with wisdom: the seven heads are seven hills on which the woman is seated; ¹⁰they are also seven kings, five of whom have fallen, one is, the other has not yet come, and when he comes he must remain only a little while. ¹¹As for the beast that was and is not, it is an eighth but it belongs to the seven, and it goes to perdition. ¹²And the ten horns that you saw are ten kings who have not yet received royal power, but they are to receive authority as kings for one hour, together with the beast. ¹³These are of one mind and give over their power and authority to the beast; ¹⁴they will make war on the Lamb, and the Lamb will conquer them, for he is Lord of lords and King of kings, and those with him are called and chosen and faithful."

15 And he said to me, "The waters that you saw, where the harlot is seated, are peoples and multitudes and nations and tongues. ¹⁶And the ten horns that you saw, they and the beast will hate the harlot; they will make her desolate and naked, and devour her flesh and burn her up with fire, ¹⁷for God has put it into their hearts to carry out his purpose by being of one mind and giving over their royal power to the beast, until the words of God shall be fulfilled. ¹⁸And the woman that you saw is the great city which has dominion over the kings of the earth."

The Fall of Babylon

18 After this I saw another angel coming down from heaven, having great authority; and the earth was made bright with his splendor. ²And he called out with a mighty voice,

"Fallen, fallen is Babylon the great!
It has become a dwelling place of demons,
a haunt of every foul spirit,
a haunt of every foul and hateful bird;
³for all nations have drunk ᵏ the wine of her
impure passion,

17:8: Dan 7:3; Rev 3:5.　**17:12:** Dan 7:20–24.　**17:14:** Dan 2:47.　**18:2:** Is 21:9; Jer 50:39.　**18:3:** Jer 25:15, 27.

17:8 was, and is not, and is to ascend: The description of the beast is a parody of the Lord's name in 1:4, 8, and 4:8. Some interpret this as an allusion to the Nero *redivivus* legend, a popular belief in the first century that Nero, despite reports of his death, had secretly escaped to Parthia and would return with an army to reclaim the Roman Empire. Ultimately, it seems to refer to the "coming" of the Antichrist at the end of time (2 Thess 2:8–10), the lawless one whom Paul calls "the son of perdition" (2 Thess 2:3). **bottomless pit:** The abyss. See note on Rev 9:1. **perdition:** The beast is destined for the lake of eternal fire (19:20). **book of life:** A heavenly registry of the saints. See note on Rev 20:12.

17:9 seven hills: A representation of Rome, the city that sprawls over seven hills, according to the writers of classical antiquity (e.g., Virgil, *Aeneid* 6, 783; Cicero, *To Atticus* 6, 5; Martial, *Epigrams* 4, 64). Many interpreters, ancient and modern alike, identify the harlot city with Rome on the basis of this tradition, though some see a reference to Jerusalem, noting that it, too, was said to rest on seven hills according to one rabbinic tradition (*Pirqe de Rabbi Eleazar* 10). Interestingly, there is reason to think that two historical referents are in view here rather than one and that Jerusalem and Rome both form part of the picture. Throughout the chapter, the apocalyptic symbolism is stacked so that the upper images (harlot-city-woman) are distinguished from the lower images (beast-hills-waters). It is thus possible to identify Jerusalem as the harlot city who joins forces with the beastly power of Rome in opposition to Christianity. See notes on Rev 17:1 and 17:16.

17:10 seven kings: Numerous interpretations of this have been offered. Read symbolically, it is said to represent all earthly kings, all the Roman emperors, or all the empires of history until the end of time. Read literally, it is often said to stand for seven Roman emperors, the sixth in succession being either Nero (A.D. 54 to 68) or Domitian (A.D. 81 to 96), both of whom were followed by emperors who ruled only a short time. For the most part, ancient Roman and Jewish authors counted Julius Caesar as the first emperor, in which case Nero is the sixth of Rome's first seven dictators (e.g., Suetonius, *Lives of the Twelve Caesars*; Josephus, *Antiquities* 18, 32; *4 Ezra* 12, 14–15).

17:12 ten kings: Presumably rulers of a lower rank than the

Caesars mentioned in 17:10. Their identity is a mystery, but their destiny is made clear in 19:17–21. **one hour:** Corresponds to the "hour" of divine judgment (14:7, 15) when the harlot city is destroyed (18:10, 17, 19).

📖 **17:16 make her . . . naked:** A public disgracing of the harlot. ● It recalls how the Lord, in OT times, punished the "brazen harlot" Jerusalem (Ezek 16:30) by sending her Gentile lovers to strip her naked and stone her (Ezek 16:35–43; 23:22–31). **burn her up with fire:** If the harlot is Jerusalem, this symbolizes the Roman conquest of the city in A.D. 70. Interpreters who see the main referent throughout the chapter as Rome (or Jerusalem) exclusively often read this in terms of self-destruction caused by infighting or civil war.

17:18 dominion: The language of political sovereignty points to a corruptive spiritual influence that leads other nations into deception (18:23). (1) If the city is Jerusalem, this could refer to the effort of official Judaism to slander the Christian movement and turn the Gentile world against it. (2) If the city is Rome, its political dominance over the Mediterranean world is in view, along with the spread of spiritual corruption through the cult of the emperors. See note on Rev 13:11.

📖✿ **18:1–24** A dirge over the death of the harlot city Babylon. ● Several images and expressions in this chapter are taken from the judgment oracles of the Prophets, especially Jeremiah's condemnation of ancient Babylon in Jer 50–51. The cry that Babylon is **fallen** (18:2) recalls Jer 51:8; the charge that nations have **drunk her wine** (18:3) recalls Jer 51:7; the call to come **out of her** (18:4) recalls Jer 50:8 and 51:45; the vision of her sins **heaped high as heaven** (18:5) recalls Jer 51:9; the judgment by **fire** (18:8) recalls Jer 50:32 and 51:30; the rejoicing of **heaven** (18:20) recalls Jer 51:48; the image of a stone hurled **into the sea** (18:21) recalls Jer 51:63–64; and scenes of the **slain** (18:24) filling the city recalls Jer 51:49. ● Babylon and the harlot, whose smoke goes up forever, are none other than the lustful, the adulterous, and the arrogant. If you wish to escape such punishments, have no desire to commit such grave sins. For in the present age, Babylon is always going to destruction and burning up in part (St. Caesarius of Arles, *Exposition of the Apocalypse*, homily 18).

18:3 drunk the wine: The maddening wine mixed in the cup of the harlot (17:4; 18:6).

ᵏ Other ancient authorities read *fallen by.*

and the kings of the earth have committed
    fornication with her,
and the merchants of the earth have grown rich
    with the wealth of her wantonness."
[4]Then I heard another voice from heaven saying,
    "Come out of her, my people,
lest you take part in her sins,
lest you share in her plagues;
[5]for her sins are heaped high as heaven,
    and God has remembered her iniquities.
[6]Render to her as she herself has rendered,
    and repay her double for her deeds;
mix a double draught for her in the cup she
    mixed.
[7]As she glorified herself and played the
    wanton,
so give her a like measure of torment and
    mourning.
Since in her heart she says, 'A queen I sit,
I am no widow, mourning I shall never see,'
[8]so shall her plagues come in a single day,
    pestilence and mourning and famine,
and she shall be burned with fire;
for mighty is the Lord God who judges her."

9 And the kings of the earth, who committed fornication and were wanton with her, will weep and wail over her when they see the smoke of her burning; [10]they will stand far off, in fear of her torment, and say,

    "Alas! alas! you great city,
    you mighty city, Babylon!
In one hour has your judgment come."

11 And the merchants of the earth weep and mourn for her, since no one buys their cargo any more, [12]cargo of gold, silver, jewels and pearls, fine linen, purple, silk and scarlet, all kinds of scented wood, all articles of ivory, all articles of costly wood, bronze, iron and marble, [13]cinnamon, spice, incense, myrrh, frankincense, wine, oil, fine flour and wheat, cattle and sheep,

---

18:4: Is 48:20; Jer 50:8.   **18:5:** Jer 51:9.
18:6: Ps 137:8.   **18:7:** Is 47:8–9.
18:9: Ezek 26:16–17.   **18:11:** Ezek 27:36.
18:12: Ezek 27:12–13, 22.

18:4 Come out of her: A call to escape the harlot city before its demise (cf. Gen 19:12-14; Tob 14:4, 8). Some read this as an echo of Jesus' warning to flee Jerusalem when the time of its judgment draws near (Lk 21:20-21). Others, identifying the city as Rome, read this as a call to escape the godless corruption of the capital, much as Paul emphasizes the moral imperative in a similar prophetic passage (2 Cor 6:17, quoting Is 52:11). **her plagues:** The divine curses of the seven seals (6:1—8:5), the seven trumpets (8:6—11:19), and the seven bowls (15:1—16:21).

18:9-19 The clients of the harlot, represented by kings (18:9), merchants (18:11), and sailors (18:17), look on in tears as the wicked city melts down in flames. They are saddened, not for her, but for themselves, being pained at the loss of their illicit pleasures and wealth. • This subsection of the chapter draws mainly from the lamentation over Tyre in Ezek 27. More than a dozen commodities listed in 18:12-13 are taken from Ezek 27:12-22.

Who Is Babylon?

THE CITY destroyed by God in the Book of Revelation goes by several names: "Babylon the great" (Rev 14:8; 17:5; 18:2, 10, 21), the "great harlot" (17:1, 15; 19:2), and the "great city" (16:19; 17:18; 18:10, 16, 18, 19, 21). Most scholars through the centuries have identified this as Rome, a city infamous in the ancient world for its power, wealth, idolatry, and immorality. In modern times, other scholars have identified the city, not as Rome, but as apostate Jerusalem, for it too had degenerated into a place of godless corruption and bloodshed by the first century. Resolving the issue depends on the date one assigns to the book, how one reads the symbolism of the book, and whether one sees the two interpretations as mutually exclusive. The main arguments in favor of both positions are considered below.

BABYLON AS ROME

The interpretation of Babylon as Rome draws support from external and internal evidence.

(1) The most ancient tradition that survives from the early Church, that of St. Irenaeus, appears to say that John received the visions of Revelation near the end of the reign of Domitian (ca. A.D. 96). If this is accepted, the harlot city must be imperial Rome, though a few have suggested that John could be looking back on the fall of Jerusalem in A.D. 70. See introduction to Revelation: *Date*.

(2) Rome is several times called "Babylon" in Jewish apocalyptic texts that date back to the early second century (e.g., *4 Ezra* 3, 1; *2 Baruch* 2, 1). The logic behind this description is precisely the fact that Rome, like Babylon of old, conquered and destroyed the city of Jerusalem. Peter also appears to use Babylon as a code name for the city of Rome (1 Pet 5:13). Conversely, no contemporary text outside the NT uses the name Babylon for Jerusalem.

(3) The harlot city of Babylon is seated on seven hills—a traditional description of the imperial city of Rome. One rabbinic tradition makes this same assertion about Jerusalem, but it dates to a time well after the NT period (see note on Rev 17:9).

(4) The harlot city is drunk with the blood of Christian martyrs and saints (Rev 17:6). This, too, is an apt description of Rome, for at least two emperors unleashed a bloody persecution against the Church in the first century, Nero and Domitian.

(5) Babylon is said to exercise dominion over many kings (Rev 17:18; 18:3) and peoples (17:15) and is pictured at the center of a vast trading empire that enriched many nations (18:11-19). Interpreted literally, these statements are easily applicable to the Roman Empire of the first century. It is less clear how these verses could be said to describe Jerusalem.

(6) Occasionally, the book describes the harlot city with the help of OT passages that refer to God's judgment on pagan cities of the past, such as Tyre (see notes on Rev 17:1-6; 18:9-19) and ancient Babylon itself (see notes on Rev 14:8; 17:1; 18:1–24). Again, Rome quite easily fits the profile of a pagan metropolis that is destined to face the wrath of the Almighty.

BABYLON AS JERUSALEM

The interpretation of Babylon as Jerusalem draws its support mainly from the internal evidence of the text, though some external evidence gives support to it as well (see introduction to Revelation: *Date*).

(1) The Book of Revelation tells us that the "great city" is the city where Jesus was crucified (11:8). Since this is the first use of the expression in the book, there is reason to think that Jerusalem is the identification intended throughout. At least, John gives no indication that more than one "great city" is in view as the book unfolds.

(2) The streets of the harlot city run red, not only with the blood of Christian martyrs and saints (17:6), but also with the blood of "prophets" (18:24). This, too, sounds like a reference to Jerusalem, a city that spilled the blood of the earliest martyrs (11:7–8; Acts 7:58; 12:2; 26:10) and had a long history of murdering God's prophets (Mt 23:37; Lk 13:33), including the Messiah (Mt 27:25–26).

(3) Babylon is portrayed as a "harlot" who seduces other nations (17:1–6). This could apply to a city such as Rome, for the OT uses this imagery for Gentile cities such as Tyre and Nineveh. However, the image of the harlot city is extensively developed in the OT with reference to Jerusalem. She was the city accused by the Prophets of prostituting herself to the nations by various transgressions of the covenant (see notes on Rev 17:1–6; 17:16; 18:22–23). Not only so, but the harlot's attire in Revelation recalls prophetic texts that describe sinful Jerusalem bedecked in the same way (see note on Rev 17:4).

(4) A voice from heaven summons the faithful to flee from sinful Babylon (18:4), lest they be destroyed by the "plagues" and "fire" that are soon to ravage the city (18:8). It is difficult to see how this fits the historical situation in Rome, a city that has maintained an uninterrupted Christian presence extending to the present day. However, in the case of Jerusalem, we know that Jesus urged his disciples to flee the city before its demise (Lk 21:20–21), and history confirms that they heeded his warning in time (Eusebius, *Ecclesiastical History* 3, 5).

(5) The harlot city is destined for a fiery destruction (17:16; 18:8, 18). This is one of many things in the book expected to take place "soon" (1:1, 3; 22:6, 7, 10, 12). Now, supposing it possible that John wrote the book in the late 60s, the burning of Jerusalem in A.D. 70 would fit the prophetic time frame perfectly (Mt 22:7). However, Rome was not set ablaze and trampled into obscurity until the city was overrun by Visigoth barbarians in A.D. 410, more than three hundred years after the warning in Revelation was issued. Confirmation that John expects an imminent fulfillment of his oracles comes near the end of the book. In contrast to the prophet Daniel, who was told to seal up the account of his visions because their fulfillment awaited a time in the distant future (Dan 12:4), John is told *not* to seal up his visions because the time of fulfillment is near (22:10). Historically, then, it is easier to account for the urgent tone of the book if the city in question is Jerusalem rather than Rome.

(6) The destruction of the harlot city (chaps. 17–18) is followed by visions of a heavenly city (chaps. 21–22). Clearly these cities are portrayed as the spiritual antithesis of one another, as several contrasting parallels show (see note on Rev 21:2). The most natural interpretation views the *new* Jerusalem, which comes down from *heaven*, as the successor to the *old* Jerusalem, which was built on *earth*, as elsewhere in the NT (Gal 4:24–27). Of course, it is not impossible that the new Jerusalem could be taken as the counterimage of Rome, as many scholars hold, but the fit is less perfect. For this involves a split antithesis that defines the heavenly city over against two different earthly cities, i.e., the celestial Jerusalem is "new" in relation to the old Jerusalem, but "heavenly" in relation to the earthly city of Rome. Strictly speaking, then, either interpretation is possible. But the new Jerusalem in heaven is more readily envisioned as the counterpart and successor to the old Jerusalem on earth.

WHAT IS curious about the above is the strength of both interpretations. Some details seem to fit a description of Rome, while others are more clearly applicable to Jerusalem. This being the case, one might argue that these opposing views are not mutually exclusive but that both are legitimate in different ways. In our judgment, a stronger case can be made for Jerusalem as the city whose demise is apocalyptically presented in Revelation. But this does not mean that other readings of the book are thereby ruled out. Jerusalem was the first city to fit the description in Revelation, but it is by no means the only city. What was true of apostate Jerusalem—that it became a center of godlessness, violence, and corruption to the point of defying God and shedding the blood of his servants—holds true of countless cities down through the ages. History is clear that Rome stood next in line to carry on the legacy of Jerusalem by its ruthless persecution of Christianity, so Revelation's warnings of divine judgment apply to it as well. Indeed, Rome's bloodguilt is very much part of the message of the book, even in its literal sense (e.g., 13:7). So even if John intended us to think first and foremost of Jerusalem, God's judgment serves as a warning to any and every city thereafter that would choose to turn against the Lord and his disciples. Thus, when one surveys the history of interpretation, it is not surprising to learn that Rome and, indeed, many other earthly powers, political as well as religious, have been identified as the Babylon of Revelation. We must not restrict the meaning of apocalyptic events to exclude later historical applications. Revelation's theological message is a timeless message, and its pastoral application is one of perennial relevance. It is as meaningful now as it was in the first century and will continue to be so till the end of time. «

horses and chariots, and slaves, that is, human souls.
¹⁴"The fruit for which your soul longed has gone from you,
    and all your delicacies and your splendor are lost to you, never to be found again!"
¹⁵The merchants of these wares, who gained wealth from her, will stand far off, in fear of her torment, weeping and mourning aloud,
¹⁶"Alas, alas, for the great city
    that was clothed in fine linen, in purple and scarlet,
    adorned with gold, with jewels, and with pearls!
¹⁷In one hour all this wealth has been laid waste."

And all shipmasters and seafaring men, sailors and all whose trade is on the sea, stood far off ¹⁸and cried out as they saw the smoke of her burning,
"What city was like the great city?"
¹⁹And they threw dust on their heads, as they wept and mourned, crying out,
"Alas, alas, for the great city
    where all who had ships at sea grew rich by her wealth!
In one hour she has been laid waste.
²⁰Rejoice over her, O heaven,
O saints and apostles and prophets,
    for God has given judgment for you against her!"

21 Then a mighty angel took up a stone like a great millstone and threw it into the sea, saying,
"So shall Babylon the great city be thrown down with violence,
    and shall be found no more;
²²and the sound of harpists and minstrels, of flute players and trumpeters,
    shall be heard in you no more;
and a craftsman of any craft
    shall be found in you no more;
and the sound of the millstone
    shall be heard in you no more;
²³and the light of a lamp
    shall shine in you no more;
and the voice of bridegroom and bride
    shall be heard in you no more;
for your merchants were the great men of the earth,
    and all nations were deceived by your sorcery.
²⁴And in her was found the blood of prophets and of saints,
    and of all who have been slain on earth."

The Rejoicing in Heaven

19 After this I heard what seemed to be the mighty voice of a great multitude in heaven, crying,
"Hallelujah! Salvation and glory and power belong to our God,
²for his judgments are true and just;
he has judged the great harlot who corrupted the earth with her fornication,
and he has avenged on her the blood of his servants."
³Once more they cried,
"Hallelujah! The smoke from her goes up for ever and ever."
⁴And the twenty-four elders and the four living creatures fell down and worshiped God who is seated on the throne, saying, "Amen. Hallelujah!"
⁵And from the throne came a voice crying,
"Praise our God, all you his servants,
you who fear him, small and great."
⁶Then I heard what seemed to be the voice of a great multitude, like the sound of many waters and like the sound of mighty thunderpeals, crying,
"Hallelujah! For the Lord our God the Almighty reigns.
⁷Let us rejoice and exult and give him the glory,
for the marriage of the Lamb has come,
and his Bride has made herself ready;
⁸it was granted her to be clothed with fine linen, bright and pure"—

18:15: Ezek 27:36, 31.   **18:17:** Is 23:14; Ezek 27:26–30.   **18:19:** Ezek 27:30–34.   **18:20:** Is 44:23; Jer 51:48.   **18:21:** Jer 51:63; Ezek 26:21.   **18:22:** Is 24:8; Ezek 26:13.   **18:23:** Jer 25:10.   **18:24:** Jer 51:49.   **19:2:** Deut 32:43.   **19:3:** Is 34:10.   **19:5:** Ps 115:13.   **19:7:** Ps 118:24.

18:16 purple . . . scarlet . . . gold . . . jewels . . . pearls: The finery of a harlot (17:4).

18:21 a great millstone: Recalls the words of Jeremiah about Babylon (Jer 51:63), as well as the teaching of Jesus about one who leads others to sin (Mt 18:6; Mk 9:42; Lk 17:2).

18:22–23 The **millstone** falling silent, the lighted **lamp** going dark, and the **bridegroom and bride** no longer heard singing are scenarios drawn from Jeremiah's oracles prophesying the desolation of Jerusalem (Jer 7:34; 16:9; 25:10).

18:24 blood of prophets . . . saints: The harlot city is a murderous city, stained with the blood of the Lord's faithful ones (17:6). **all . . . slain on earth:** A prophetic hyperbole, stressing that the city's bloodguilt has reached an extreme level. ● The wording is borrowed from Jer 51:49, where "the slain of all the earth" were said to have fallen in Babylon.

19:2 avenged . . . the blood: In answer to the pleas and petitions of the martyrs in 6:9–10 (CCC 2642).

19:4 twenty-four elders: Heavenly saints. See note on Rev 4:4. **four living creatures:** Heavenly angels. See note on Rev 4:6.

19:7–9 Christ and the Church are forever united in a covenant of marital love. In one sense, this is a present reality for the Church, who is joined to the Bridegroom by the grace of Baptism (Eph 5:22–32); but it is also a future hope, inasmuch as that union will reach perfection in the glory of heaven (Mt 25:1–13). John envisions the Church dressed in a bridal gown sewn by a life of purity and righteousness. Later, the Bride of the Lamb is described as the heavenly Jerusalem, the virgin city gilded with gold and adorned with precious stones (21:9–21) (CCC 757, 865). ● The marriage of the bridal city recalls Ezek 16:8–14, where the Lord joined himself in wedlock to ancient Jerusalem, having cleansed her in water and clothed

for the fine linen is the righteous deeds of the saints.

9 And the angel said[1] to me, "Write this: Blessed are those who are invited to the marriage supper of the Lamb." And he said to me, "These are true words of God." [10]Then I fell down at his feet to worship him, but he said to me, "You must not do that! I am a fellow servant with you and your brethren who hold the testimony of Jesus. Worship God." For the testimony of Jesus is the spirit of prophecy.

The Rider on the White Horse

11 Then I saw heaven opened, and behold, a white horse! He who sat upon it is called Faithful and True, and in righteousness he judges and makes war. [12]His eyes are like a flame of fire, and on his head are many diadems; and he has a name inscribed which no one knows but himself. [13]He is clothed in a robe dipped in[m] blood, and the name by which he is called is The Word of God. [14]And the armies of heaven, wearing fine linen, white and pure, followed him on white horses. [15]From his mouth issues a sharp sword with which to strike the nations, and he will rule them with a rod of iron; he will tread the wine press of the fury of the wrath of God the Almighty. [16]On his robe and on his thigh he has a name inscribed, King of kings and Lord of lords.

The Beast and Its Armies Defeated

17 Then I saw an angel standing in the sun, and with a loud voice he called to all the birds that fly in midheaven, "Come, gather for the great supper of God, [18]to eat the flesh of kings, the flesh of captains, the flesh of mighty men, the flesh of horses and their riders, and the flesh of all men, both free and slave, both small and great." [19]And I saw the beast and the kings of the earth with their armies gathered to make war against him who sits upon the horse and against his army. [20]And the beast was captured, and with it the false prophet who in its presence had worked the signs by which he deceived those who had received the mark of the beast and those who worshiped its image. These two were thrown alive into the lake of fire that burns with

---

19:11: Ezek 1:1.　**19:12:** Dan 10:6.　**19:15:** Ps 2:9.　**19:16:** Deut 10:17; Dan 2:47.　**19:17:** Ezek 39:4, 17–20.

---

her in gold, jewelry, and fine linen. Similar images of glorified Zion appear in Is 61:10 and 62:5.

19:9 Blessed are those: The fourth of seven beatitudes in Revelation. See note on Rev 1:3.

19:10 Worship God: The worship of any created thing is idolatry. John, of course, is not an idolater but is overcome by the heavenly glory radiating from the angel (22:8–9). He receives no such rebuke when he falls prostrate before the glorified Christ (1:17).

19:11–21 Christ appears as the warrior Messiah, riding into battle with a full cavalry of angels trailing behind him. His mission: to execute judgment on the beast and the false prophet who allied themselves against him and his followers. This is the battle of Armageddon, for which preparations were made in 16:14–16. ● The depiction of Christ dressed in a robe covered with **blood** (19:13) and treading the **wine press** of wrath (19:15) recalls Is 63:1–6, where the Lord marches forth to war, his garments splattered with enemy blood and his feet stomping down the nations in a wine press. The depiction of Christ as the **Word** (19:13) who swings a sharp **sword** (19:15) recalls Wis 18:15–16, where the divine word leaps down from heaven as a warrior armed with a sword.

19:12 many diadems: Jesus is crowned with many crowns, symbolizing the plentitude of his royal authority as "King of kings" (19:16). **a name inscribed:** Either on his crowns or possibly on his forehead, like the saints who bear his name (14:1).

19:13 The Word of God: Jesus, the divine Word of the Father (Jn 1:1), enacts the divine word of judgment (Jn 5:22) against those who reject his gospel (Jn 12:48).

19:15 a rod of iron: The scepter of the Davidic Messiah (Ps 2:9). See note on Rev 12:5.

19:17–21 Jesus condemns his enemies to a dreadful destiny. The judgment in question is spiritual, leading to the eternal **lake of fire**, though it is possible that historical events of the first century lie in the background. For instance, the overthrow of the **beast** may be linked to the suicide of Nero in A.D. 68. Not only was his name the number of the beast (note on Rev 13:18), but he had waged a violent war against the Church (11:7; 13:7). Likewise, the judgment of the **false prophet** may be linked to the massacre of Judea's religious leadership in the first Jewish revolt against Rome (A.D. 67 to 70). So understood, this is a vision of divine punishment being imposed on the first persecutors of Christianity. Ultimately, however, it foreshadows the final battle of history, when Christ returns and destroys the powers of evil once and for all (20:7–10; 2 Thess 1:5–10; 2:1–12). ● The imagery of the **great supper** comes from the apocalyptic war scenes of Ezek 38–39. After the Lord destroys those who assault his people, birds are invited to gorge themselves on the flesh and blood of fallen enemies strewn across the battlefield (Ezek 39:17–20).

19:20 the lake of fire: The molten sea of hell, where the damned are destined to writhe in everlasting torment (21:8). Eventually the devil himself will be hurled into its flames (20:10) (CCC 1033–37).

Word Study

Hallelujah (Rev 19:1, 3, 4, 6)

Hallēluïa (Gk.): A transliteration of two Hebrew terms meaning "Praise the Lord!" It occurs only four times in the NT but is often used in the OT as a liturgical acclamation, especially in the Psalter. Certain psalms, for instance, are framed by this expression, which serves as an opening and closing line (Ps 135, 146–50). It is also a recurrent acclamation in the Hallel Psalms that were traditionally sung during the Jewish Passover meal (Ps 113–18). Some scholars thus maintain that the Passover liturgy is the background of the repeated "Hallelujah" in Rev 19:1–6, since the song builds up to the "marriage supper of the Lamb" (Rev 19:9). This is the triumphal banquet celebrated by the redeemed of the new Exodus, saved by the blood of Christ, the new Passover Lamb (Rev 5:6–10; 15:2–3). The "Hallelujah" has since passed into the liturgical vocabulary of the Church, where the Eucharist is celebrated as a memorial of the new Exodus accomplished through Christ (CCC 1340).

---

[1] Greek *he said.*
[m] Other ancient authorities read *sprinkled with.*

brimstone. [21]And the rest were slain by the sword of him who sits upon the horse, the sword that issues from his mouth; and all the birds were gorged with their flesh.

The Thousand Years

20 Then I saw an angel coming down from heaven, holding in his hand the key of the bottomless pit and a great chain. [2]And he seized the dragon, that ancient serpent, who is the Devil and Satan, and bound him for a thousand years, [3]and threw him into the pit, and shut it and sealed it over him, that he should deceive the nations no more, till the thousand years were ended. After that he must be let out for a little while.

4 Then I saw thrones, and seated on them were those to whom judgment was committed. Also I saw the souls of those who had been beheaded for their testimony to Jesus and for the word of God, and who had not worshiped the beast or its image and had not received its mark on their foreheads or

their hands. They came to life, and reigned with Christ a thousand years. [5]The rest of the dead did not come to life until the thousand years were ended. This is the first resurrection. [6]Blessed and holy is he who shares in the first resurrection! Over such the second death has no power, but they shall be priests of God and of Christ, and they shall reign with him a thousand years.

Satan's Doom

7 And when the thousand years are ended, Satan will be released from his prison [8]and will come out to deceive the nations which are at the four corners of the earth, that is, Gog and Ma'gog, to gather them for battle; their number is like the sand of the sea. [9]And they marched up over the broad earth and surrounded the camp of the saints and the beloved city; but fire came down from heaven [n] and consumed them, [10]and the devil who had deceived them was thrown into the lake of fire and brimstone where the beast and the false

---

20:4: Dan 7:9, 22, 27.   **20:8:** Ezek 38:2, 9, 15.   **20:9:** 2 Kings 1:10–12.

20:1–6 The binding of Satan and the millennial reign of Christ. Three views of the millennium have dominated theological discussion over the centuries. (1) *Premillennialism* is the view that Christ, when he comes again, will establish his reign on earth for 1,000 years. Also called *chiliasm* (from the Greek word for "one thousand"), this interpretation was popular in the second and third centuries (e.g., St. Justin Martyr, *Dialogue with Trypho* 80). A modern version, advanced by Protestant dispensationalists, holds that the Church will be gathered into heaven at the Second Coming, after which Christ will restore the theocratic kingdom of David in Jerusalem for 1000 years and fulfill all of God's promises to ethnic Israel. (2) *Postmillennialism* interprets the 1000 years as symbolizing that period of history during which the gospel goes forth and gradually has its full effect of Christianizing the world. Once this global process is complete, Christ will return in glory. Advocates generally hold that the length of the millennium is beyond our ability to calculate. (3) *Amillennialism*, like postmillennialism, holds to a symbolic view of the 1000 years and does not envision Christ reigning on earth in visible form. The millennium is said to represent the entire stretch of history between the First and Second Coming, that time when Christ reigns in a spiritual and sacramental way through the Church. Rising to prominence in the fourth and fifth centuries, this has probably been the most widely held view among Catholic theologians throughout history (beginning with St. Augustine, *City of God* 20, 9). ● The background of the millennium may be traced to the period of the Davidic covenant, which was established almost exactly 1000 years before the coming of Christ. This age began with David extending his rule over Israel and other nations (2 Sam 5–8) and with Solomon instructing the nations in the ways of righteousness (1 Kings 10:1–10, 23–24). It is also a time when the faithful of Israel first experienced martyrdom for their faith (Dan 3:16–23; 2 Mac 7:1–42). The images in 20:1 also have links with Davidic traditions: the **key** recalls the key of David in 3:7; the **pit** of the netherworld was believed to be sealed off by the foundation stone of Solomon's Temple; and the **chain** that prevents deception may reflect the tradition that a chain hung in Solomon's courtroom and was used to verify the truthfulness of testimony given under oath. These and other features of the Davidic age prefigure the messianic age, during which Christ reigns over the Church and the world as the royal Davidic Messiah. ● The Catholic Church rejects all forms of millenarianism (i.e., *chiliasm*), which contends that Christ will come again to establish a visible kingdom on earth and to inaugurate a golden age of peace and prosperity within human history (Decree of the Holy Office, 1944) (CCC 676).

20:1 the bottomless pit: Or, "the abyss". See note on Rev 9:1.

20:2 that ancient serpent: The devil as disguised in Gen 3:1–14 and exposed in 12:9.

20:4 I saw thrones: A heavenly court, or possibly the thrones of apostolic government in the Church, as in Mt 19:28 and Lk 22:28–30. ● The scene recalls Dan 7:9–11, where the beast from the sea is condemned and thrown into the fire, and Dan 7:26–27, where the kingdom of the Son of man is given to the saints. **beheaded for their testimony:** Martyrs such as John the Baptist (Mk 6:27) and the apostles James (Acts 12:1–2) and Paul (Christian tradition). These and others killed for their faith reign with Christ in a special way (Rev 20:6), even though all believers share in the royal-priestly reign of Christ, whether in heaven (Rev 2:26–27) or on earth (Rev 5:10).

20:5 the first resurrection: The meaning of the two resurrections is uncertain. The first may refer to a spiritual resurrection to new life through faith and Baptism (Jn 5:25; Rom 6:3–4), followed by a bodily resurrection at the return of Christ (Jn 5:28–29; 1 Thess 4:15–16). Or perhaps both resurrections are bodily, the first being that of Christ and the saints of the OT (Mt 27:52–53) and the second involving the rest of humanity Rev (20:12–13; 1 Cor 15:22).

20:6 Blessed: The fifth of seven beatitudes in Revelation. See note on Rev 1:3. **the second death:** The spiritual death of hell (20:14). The first death is bodily death (20:5).

20:8 Gog and Magog: Names that symbolize the coalition of evil nations summoned by Satan to besiege the Church of the last days. This will be the final explosion of the devil's fury before his consignment to hell (20:10). ● The two names come from the apocalyptic war vision of Ezek 38–39, where Gog and the land of Magog assemble an international army to plunder the beloved People of God. Their plans are foiled, however, when fire and brimstone rain down from the Lord and destroy them (Rev 20:9).

20:9 camp of the saints: Like the Exodus generation of Israel, the pilgrim Church on earth is still journeying toward the rest of the Promised Land. **the beloved city:** Another image for the Church, this time pictured as the heavenly Jerusalem (21:2).

20:10 the lake of fire: Hell, where the devil joins his former agents, burning since 19:20. **tormented:** The damned are not

---

[n] Other ancient authorities read *from God, out of heaven,* or *out of heaven from God.*

prophet were, and they will be tormented day and night for ever and ever.

The Dead Are Judged

11 Then I saw a great white throne and him who sat upon it; from his presence earth and sky fled away, and no place was found for them. [12]And I saw the dead, great and small, standing before the throne, and books were opened. Also another book was opened, which is the book of life. And the dead were judged by what was written in the books, by what they had done. [13]And the sea gave up the dead in it, Death and Hades gave up the dead in them, and all were judged by what they had done. [14]Then Death and Hades were thrown into the lake of fire. This is the second death, the lake of fire; [15]and if any one's name was not found written in the book of life, he was thrown into the lake of fire.

The New Heaven and the New Earth

21 Then I saw a new heaven and a new earth; for the first heaven and the first earth had passed away, and the sea was no more. [2]And I saw the holy city, new Jerusalem, coming down out of heaven from God, prepared as a bride adorned for her husband; [3]and I heard a great voice from the throne saying, "Behold, the dwelling of God is with men. He will dwell with them, and they shall be his people,° and God himself will be with them;ᴾ [4]he will wipe away every tear from their eyes, and death shall be no more, neither shall there be mourning nor crying nor pain any more, for the former things have passed away."

5 And he who sat upon the throne said, "Behold, I make all things new." Also he said, "Write this, for these words are trustworthy and true." [6]And he said to me, "It is done! I am the Alpha and the

---

20:11–12: Dan 7:9–10. **20:15:** Rev 3:5. **21:1:** Is 66:22. **21:2:** Rev 3:12. **21:3:** Ezek 37:27. **21:4:** Is 25:8; 35:10. **21:5:** Is 43:19. **21:6:** Is 55:1.

---

annihilated or disintegrated, but kept alive to be tortured for eternity (Mt 25:46; Mk 9:47–48).

20:11–15 The Last Judgment, when the souls of the dead are rejoined to their bodies (the second resurrection) to stand before Christ the Judge. Their secrets will be revealed, and every thought, word, and deed catalogued in the heavenly books will be reviewed. This is the Last Day, when both the righteous and the wicked will be raised (Acts 24:15) and sent their separate ways (Dan 12:2; Mt 25:31–46; Jn 5:29) (CCC 677, 1038–41).

20:11 great white throne: The judgment seat of Christ (2 Cor 5:10), the description of which recalls the ivory throne of Solomon (1 Kings 10:18). Elsewhere in Revelation, Jesus appears with white hair (1:14), wears a white garment (3:5), moves on a white cloud (14:14), and rides a white horse (19:11). The angels and saints are also robed in white (4:4; 6:11; 7:9; 15:6; 19:14).

20:12 the book of life: A listing of all the saints destined for glory (3:5). It will be opened for the final roll call of the righteous at the Last Judgment, with the names of the saved read aloud (21:27) and the names of damned nowhere to be found (20:15). ● The book of life is a metaphor based on a comparison with human affairs. For it is common practice among men to inscribe in a book those who are chosen for an office. Now, since all the predestined are chosen by God for eternal life, the enrollment of the predestined is called the book of life (St. Thomas Aquinas, *Summa Theologiae*, I, 24, 1).

20:13 Death and Hades: See notes on Rev 6:8 and 9:1.

20:14 the second death: The state of spiritual death and damnation (20:6).

21:1–22:5 The final vision of the book unveils the Bride of the Lamb, the heavenly city of Jerusalem, which awaits the saints. It depicts the state of glory in terms of a marital union (21:2), a holy city (21:10), a divine temple (21:22), and a garden of paradise (22:2).

21:1 new heaven . . . new earth: Not entirely new, but entirely renewed (21:5). John sees all creation transformed and made radiant with the glory of God. It is no longer a world subject to death and decay and suffering the damaging effects of human sin (Gen 3:17–18; Rom 8:20–22). The process of cosmic regeneration has begun in the New Covenant as believers are made part of the new creation in Christ (2 Cor 5:17), but John is presented with heaven and earth once this process is complete (CCC 1042–48). ● The imagery comes from Isaiah, who prophesies a new beginning for Israel and the world in terms of a new creation (Is 65:17). He envisions this in connection with the universal worship of the Lord by all flesh (Is 66:22–23). **the sea was no more:** The abode of death and evil will be drained away (13:1; 20:13; 21:4). In apocalyptic and poetic texts, the sea often represents chaos and the habitation of all things dreadful and demonic (Job 7:12; Ps 74:13; Is 27:1; Dan 7:3).

21:2 new Jerusalem: The heavenly city, whose builder and maker is God (Heb 11:10). It touches down to earth so that the worshiping Church can join in the heavenly liturgy of the angels and saints, who never cease to praise the Lord and the Lamb (Heb 12:22–25). Visions of this eternal liturgy punctuate the Book of Revelation (4:1—5:14; 7:9—8:5; 11:15–19; 14:1–5; 15:1–8) (CCC 757). Also, there are several antithetical parallels between the new Jerusalem and the harlot city stricken with judgment in chaps. 17–18. **(1)** In 17:1, John is invited by an angel to "come" and see the harlot; in 21:9, he is invited by an angel to "come" and see the heavenly city. **(2)** In 17:3, John is carried by the Spirit to see the wicked city in the wilderness; in 21:10, he is carried by the Spirit to see the holy city from a high mountain. **(3)** In 17:4, the woman city is dressed like a prostitute, wearing gold, jewels, and pearls; in 21:11, 18, and 21, the woman city is adorned like a virgin bride, bedecked with gold, jewels, and gates made of pearl. **(4)** In 18:2, Babylon appears as a dwelling place of demons; in 21:3, the new Jerusalem appears as the dwelling place of God. **(5)** In 18:7, Babylon is accused of glorifying herself; in 21:23, the new city is wrapped in the glory of God. **(6)** In 18:23, the harlot city deceives the nations with her sorcery; in 21:24, the holy city leads the nations by her light. **prepared as a bride:** The Church is made ready for her everlasting union with Christ the Bridegroom. See note on Rev 19:7–9.

21:3–4 The saints look forward to a joyous and painless existence with God. ● The hope that God will **dwell** with **his people** restates the promise of the New Covenant in Ezek 37:27. The wiping away of **every tear** and the elimination of **death** recall the vision of the messianic banquet in Is 25:8.

21:3 the dwelling: Or, "the Tabernacle" (15:5).

21:6 the Alpha . . . the Omega: God created all things in the beginning, and he calls them back to himself in the end. See note on Rev 1:8. **the water of life:** The supernatural life of the Spirit (Jn 4:14; 7:37–39; 1 Cor 12:13). Note the contrast with Rev 21:8—here the saints are refreshed with living water; there the wicked are scorched with deadly fire (CCC 694).

° Other ancient authorities read *peoples.*
ᴾ Other ancient authorities add *and be their God.*

Omega, the beginning and the end. To the thirsty I will give water without price from the fountain of the water of life. [7]He who conquers shall have this heritage, and I will be his God and he shall be my son. [8]But as for the cowardly, the faithless, the polluted, as for murderers, fornicators, sorcerers, idolaters, and all liars, their lot shall be in the lake that burns with fire and brimstone, which is the second death."

Vision of the New Jerusalem

9 Then came one of the seven angels who had the seven bowls full of the seven last plagues, and spoke to me, saying, "Come, I will show you the Bride, the wife of the Lamb." [10]And in the Spirit he carried me away to a great, high mountain, and showed me the holy city Jerusalem coming down out of heaven from God, [11]having the glory of God, its radiance like a most rare jewel, like a jasper, clear as crystal. [12]It had a great, high wall, with twelve gates, and at the gates twelve angels, and on the gates the names of the twelve tribes of the sons of Israel were inscribed; [13]on the east three gates, on the north three gates, on the south three gates, and on the west three gates. [14]And the wall of the city had twelve foundations, and on them the twelve names of the twelve apostles of the Lamb.

15 And he who talked to me had a measuring rod of gold to measure the city and its gates and walls. [16]The city lies foursquare, its length the same as its breadth; and he measured the city with his rod, twelve thousand stadia;[q] its length and breadth and height are equal. [17]He also measured its wall, a hundred and forty-four cubits by a man's measure, that is, an angel's. [18]The wall was built of jasper, while the city was pure gold, clear as glass. [19]The foundations of the wall of the city were adorned with every jewel; the first was jasper, the second sapphire, the third agate, the fourth emerald, [20]the fifth onyx, the sixth carnelian, the seventh chrysolite, the eighth beryl, the ninth topaz, the tenth chrysoprase, the eleventh jacinth, the twelfth amethyst. [21]And the twelve gates were twelve pearls, each of the gates made of a single pearl, and the street of the city was pure gold, transparent as glass.

22 And I saw no temple in the city, for its temple is the Lord God the Almighty and the Lamb. [23]And the city has no need of sun or moon to shine upon it, for the glory of God is its light, and its lamp is the Lamb. [24]By its light shall the nations walk; and the kings of the earth shall bring their glory into it, [25]and its gates shall never be shut by day—and there shall be no night there; [26]they shall bring into it the glory and the honor of the nations. [27]But nothing unclean shall enter it, nor any one who practices abomination or falsehood, but only those who are written in the Lamb's book of life.

River of the Water of Life

22 Then he showed me the river of the water of life, bright as crystal, flowing from

---

21:7: Ps 89:27–28. **21:8:** Is 30:33. **21:10:** Ezek 40:2. **21:12:** Ezek 48:30–35; Ex 28:21. **21:15:** Ezek 40:5. **21:19:** Is 54:11–12. **21:23:** Is 24:23; 60:1, 19. **21:25:** Is 60:11. **21:27:** Is 52:1; Rev 3:5.

21:7 he shall be my son: The words of 2 Sam 7:14. • The promise of divine sonship was made to David's royal heirs and is ultimately fulfilled in Christ as the Davidic Messiah (Rom 1:3–4; Heb 1:5). Believers become sons and daughters of God by grace (Rom 8:15–16), but the full blessing of divine sonship awaits the resurrection of the saints and the glorification of their bodies, an event that coincides with the renewal of the cosmos (Rom 8:21–23).

21:8 the second death: The spiritual death of the wicked (20:14). For similar lists of damning vices, see 1 Cor 6:9–10 and Gal 5:19–21.

21:9—22:5 A dazzling description of the heavenly Jerusalem. • The vision draws from the architectural blueprint of the glorified Temple-city in Ezek 40–48. The city is seen from a **high mountain** (21:10; Ezek 40:2); it is filled with divine **glory** (21:11; Ezek 43:5); it has twelve **gates** named after the **sons of Israel** (21:12; Ezek 48:30–34); it is measured with a **measuring rod** (21:15; Ezek 40:3); its dimensions are **foursquare** (21:16; Ezek 42:15–19); it is the place of God's **throne** (22:1; Ezek 43:7); and it is the source of life-giving **water** (22:1; Ezek 47:1–9), which causes the trees along its banks to bear fruit **each month** and put forth **healing** leaves (22:2; Ezek 47:12). Other visions of Jerusalem adorned with **gold** and **every jewel** (21:18–21) are found in Tob 13:16–17 and Is 54:11–12, and as a city bathed in **light** with **gates** always open (21:23–25) in Is 60:1–3, 11.

21:10 in the Spirit: On this expression, see note on Rev 17:3.

21:14 the twelve apostles: The apostolic foundations laid by Christ (Mt 16:18; Eph 2:20). Inscribed with the names of the OT tribes and the NT apostles, heaven is the dwelling of all the righteous of covenant history.

21:16 length . . . breadth . . . height are equal: The eternal city is pictured as an enormous cube, each side measuring nearly 1,500 miles and its walls measuring over 200 feet thick. • The city is modeled after the innermost room of the Temple, the Holy of Holies, which was an all-gold chamber with a cubic shape (1 Kings 6:20).

21:22 its temple is the Lord: The Trinity is the sanctuary of the heavenly city, which is encompassed by the Father (Lord) and the Son (Lamb) and filled with the glory of the Spirit (light). If the old Jerusalem was built around the Temple, the new Jerusalem stands within a Temple, and one that no longer has partitions or veils to prevent access. In theological terms, this means that communion with God in heaven will be unmediated, exceeding in closeness and directness the access to God's presence once enjoyed in the sanctuary of Israel.

22:1 the water of life: Symbolic of the Spirit flowing through the main street of the city (21:6; Jn 7:38–39). • The imagery alludes to the river of Eden (Gen 2:10), the river that gladdens the city of God (Ps 46:4), and the fountain of living water springing from Jerusalem (Zech 14:8). For the primary allusion to Ezek 47:1–9, see note on Rev 21:9—22:5. • The water issuing from the Lord and the Lamb is an apocalyptic expression of a trinitarian mystery: in eternity, the Spirit proceeds from the Father and the Son. See note on Jn 15:26. • A single stream issues from the throne of God, and that is the grace of the Holy Spirit in the stream of the Scriptures. That stream has two banks, the Old Testament and the New, and the tree planted on either side is Christ (St. Jerome, *Tractate on the Psalms* 1). **the throne:** According to 3:21, the Father and the Son share the same throne.

---

[q] About fifteen hundred miles.

the throne of God and of the Lamb [2]through the middle of the street of the city; also, on either side of the river, the tree of life [r] with its twelve kinds of fruit, yielding its fruit each month; and the leaves of the tree were for the healing of the nations. [3]There shall no more be anything accursed, but the throne of God and of the Lamb shall be in it, and his servants shall worship him; [4]they shall see his face, and his name shall be on their foreheads. [5]And night shall be no more; they need no light of lamp or sun, for the Lord God will be their light, and they shall reign for ever and ever.

6 And he said to me, "These words are trustworthy and true. And the Lord, the God of the spirits of the prophets, has sent his angel to show his servants what must soon take place. [7]And behold, I am coming soon."

Blessed is he who keeps the words of the prophecy of this book.

Epilogue and Benediction

8 I John am he who heard and saw these things. And when I heard and saw them, I fell down to worship at the feet of the angel who showed them to me; [9]but he said to me, "You must not do that! I am a fellow servant with you and your brethren the prophets, and with those who keep the words of this book. Worship God."

10 And he said to me, "Do not seal up the words of the prophecy of this book, for the time is near.

[11]Let the evildoer still do evil, and the filthy still be filthy, and the righteous still do right, and the holy still be holy."

12 "Behold, I am coming soon, bringing my recompense, to repay every one for what he has done. [13]I am the Alpha and the Omega, the first and the last, the beginning and the end."

14 Blessed are those who wash their robes, [s] that they may have the right to the tree of life and that they may enter the city by the gates. [15]Outside are the dogs and sorcerers and fornicators and murderers and idolaters, and every one who loves and practices falsehood.

16 "I Jesus have sent my angel to you with this testimony for the churches. I am the root and the offspring of David, the bright morning star."

17 The Spirit and the Bride say, "Come." And let him who hears say, "Come." And let him who is thirsty come, let him who desires take the water of life without price.

18 I warn every one who hears the words of the prophecy of this book: if any one adds to them, God will add to him the plagues described in this book, [19]and if any one takes away from the words of the book of this prophecy, God will take away his share in the tree of life and in the holy city, which are described in this book.

20 He who testifies to these things says, "Surely I am coming soon." Amen. Come, Lord Jesus!

21 The grace of the Lord Jesus be with all the saints. [t] Amen.

22:2: Gen 2:9.   **22:3:** Zech 14:11.   **22:4:** Ps 17:15.   **22:11:** Dan 12:10.   **22:12:** Is 40:10; Jer 17:10.
22:13: Is 44:6; 48:12.   **22:14:** Gen 2:9; 3:22.   **22:16:** Is 11:1, 10.   **22:17:** Is 55:1.   **22:21:** 2 Thess 3:18

22:2 the tree of life: The reappearance of this tree, not seen in the Bible since Gen 3:24, hints that heaven is the celestial counterpart to Eden, i.e., a place of intimate fellowship with God, uncorrupted by sin and death. See note on Rev 2:7.

22:4 shall see his face: The direct vision of God is the great hope of biblical spirituality (Ps 11:7; 42:2) and the preeminent blessing of heaven (Mt 5:8; 1 Cor 13:12). Seeing the face of God points to a profound personal intimacy with him; it is an experience of knowing God that is the fulfillment of human existence. Tradition calls this the Beatific Vision (CCC 1023–28).

22:6-9 The book draws to a close by restating ideas from the introduction (1:1-3). Once again, the sense that Christ is fast approaching dominates the tone (22:6-7, 10, 12, 20). See note on Rev 1:1.

22:7 I am coming soon: Jesus is speaking, as also in 22:12 and 22:20. **Blessed:** The sixth of seven beatitudes in Revelation. See note on Rev 1:3.

22:8 I John: Probably John the Apostle. See introduction: *Author*.

22:9 Worship God: Recalls the earlier incident in 19:10.

22:10 Do not seal up: John is forbidden to seal the scroll shut. The urgency of his message makes reading it a top priority for his churches. ● This is in deliberate contrast to Dan 12:4, where the prophet was instructed to seal up his

prophecy because the time of its fulfillment was still in the distant future.

22:13 the Alpha . . . the Omega: Christ gives himself the same title given to God in 1:8, showing that he, too, is the divine Lord over history and the world.

22:14 Blessed: The last of seven beatitudes in Revelation. See note on Rev 1:3.

22:15 Outside: The heavenly city is protected from sinful contamination, with evildoers kept far outside its walls.

22:16 the root and the offspring: Jesus is the Davidic Messiah (5:5). ● The heir to David's throne is called the "root" of Jesse in Is 11:10 and the "offspring" of David in 2 Sam 7:12. **morning star:** See notes on Rev 2:28 and 2 Pet 1:19.

22:17 the Bride: The Church wedded to Christ (19:7-8). She joins the Spirit in summoning the world to salvation (CCC 2550).

22:18-19 A warning not to tamper with the Book of Revelation, whose contents were carefully dictated by heavenly visions (1:11). Strictly speaking, this is not a general warning against tampering with the Bible, though that, too, is certainly wrong. Moreover, it does not exclude the possibility that there may be Christian revelation outside the books of Scripture, such as in unwritten traditions handed down by the apostles (1 Cor 11:2; 2 Thess 2:15). ● Moses used similar words to caution Israel against adding or subtracting from the Book of Deuteronomy (Deut 4:2).

22:20 Come, Lord Jesus!: The cry of the saints, who long for Christ's return. It is probably connected with the liturgical acclamation in 1 Cor 16:22, preserved in Aramaic as *marana tha*, "Our Lord, come!" (CCC 451, 671).

---

[r] Or *the Lamb. In the midst of the street of the city, and on either side of the river, was the tree of life*, etc.
[s] Other ancient authorities read *do his commandments*.
[t] Other ancient authorities omit *all*; others omit *the saints*.

STUDY QUESTIONS: REVELATION

Chapter 1

For understanding
1. **Word Study: Revelation (1:1).** What does the Greek word *apokalypsis* mean? As used in the Bible, to what does it always refer? How can mysteries be unveiled? Why is the title *Revelation* an apt one for this particular book?
2. **1:1.** How is the message of Revelation mediated? What does the note of immediacy in the book indicate about its fulfillment? What does the connection with the Book of Daniel imply for the meaning of Revelation?
3. **1:7.** How is the towering expectation of Christ's coming in Revelation envisioned in the Book of Daniel? In the Book of Zechariah? How does John blend these two visions into one? What events, historical and eschatological, signal its fulfillment?
4. **1:12-17.** What does the inaugural vision of Revelation describe? How does this depiction of Jesus recall the visions of Daniel and Ezekiel? What is John's response?
5. **1:12.** What are the seven golden lampstands? What do they symbolize? What image from Zechariah do the lampstands evoke, and of what is it a reminder for John?

For application
1. **1:3.** When Scripture is read aloud during the liturgy, do you hear it as just another spiritual reading or as the Word of God that you are called to apply to your life? What blessing might be yours if you follow the latter approach?
2. **1:7.** What practical effect does the promise of Jesus' return at the end of time (the Parousia) have on how you live your life? How near or remote is it to you? How does it affect your faith?
3. **1:10.** Read the note for this verse. Do you regularly set aside time for personal prayer? How much time do you usually devote to it and how often? If you take time for personal prayer, what effect does it have on your relationship with God? If you do not take time for personal prayer, how might you best begin to do so?
4. **1:16.** What does the image of a "sharp two-edged sword" coming from Jesus' mouth suggest to you? Why is the detail that the sword has two sharp edges important?

Chapter 2

For understanding
1. **2:1–3:22.** Where are the seven churches in relation to each other? How can we view John's letters to them in the five ways mentioned: traditionally, geographically, structurally, spiritually, and historically?
2. **2:6.** Who were the Nicolaitans? What is John's concern about them?
3. **2:7.** To what does the repeated expression "him who conquers" refer? What do the seven letters reveal? What does the "tree of life" signify? How is this promise a subtle one in connection with Ephesus? What is its significance in relation to Christ?
4. **2:9.** Why does John refer to members of a "synagogue of Satan"? What did the exemption of Jews from the worship of the emperors have to do with their relationship with Christians? What kind of crime was the Christian refusal to acknowledge the deity of Caesar?
5. **2:14.** To what does the "teaching of Balaam" refer here? What was the role of Balaam in Num 22–24? What does Christ's warning about the perpetrators of these sins have to do with Balaam's fate?

For application

1. **2:2-5.** According to these verses, why is orthodoxy in belief not enough? Since these verses are addressed to a local church (though individual Christians should take note), how can a community repent of a falling away from the love it once had? What might the consequences be of remaining orthodox but loveless?

2. **2:9-11.** How would you encourage a person or group whose current trials were obviously going to get worse before they got better? Have you been through similar situations? What do these verses ask of the Christian, and what hope do they offer?

3. **2:14-17.** How do you think the "teaching of Balaam" and the laxity of the Nicolaitans apply to the present-day Church? How might a stronger devotion to the Eucharist help the situation? If a "new name" in Scripture means a new identity, how should that identity affect the life of the Church on earth?

4. **2:19-20.** How might an active, vibrant Christian community be susceptible to the influence of a charismatic figure who would lead it astray? What complaint does the Spirit have against such a community? According to v. 25, what should the community do?

Chapter 3

For understanding

1. **3:4.** By whom are white garments worn? What do they symbolize? Why will many in Sardis not be clothed in white garments?

2. **3:7.** Where was ancient Philadelphia, and what was the city like? What is the "key of David", and what does it have to do with Jesus? What does Is 22:22 say about this key? What does the image of the key imply in this passage from Revelation?

3. **3:12.** What does it mean to be a "pillar in the temple"? With what does the stability of the pillar contrast? Why are the faithful marked with the name of God?

4. **3:16.** What is the connection between the temperature of Laodicea's water and the fervor of its Christians?

For application

1. **3:1-2.** Visible enthusiasm or lack of it aside, what are some criteria for recognizing from its works when a community is spiritually dead? (Hint: Reflect on 1 Cor 13, Gal 5:13-25, or Jas 2.) How might a spiritually dead community return to life?

2. **3:2.** By contrast, how would one recognize a community, regardless of its size or wealth or organization, that is spiritually alive?

3. **3:10-11.** What are some of the advantages and some of the dangers in parish or community renewal programs? How can a parish or community "hold fast" to its spiritual heritage without becoming stodgy? How can it make changes without losing what it has?

4. **3:15-20.** What are some of the dangers of prosperity for individuals or groups? According to these verses, why is it *not* a disadvantage for a person or group to experience hard times? What does a person or group who is undergoing difficult times need to do about the situation, according to v. 20?

Chapter 4

For understanding
1. **4:1—5:14.** How does the third phase of the Book of Revelation begin? What happens in these chapters? What is their dual focus? How does the liturgical setting in heaven allude to the cultic figures and fixtures of the Jerusalem Temple? What ancient belief do these and similar scenes express about the Temple?
2. **4:4.** Whom do the 24 elders represent? Upon what is the symbolism based?
3. **4:6.** What are the "four living creatures"? What do they symbolize? How does their appearance resemble the visions of Isaiah and Ezekiel? How does tradition connect these creatures with the four evangelists?
4. **4:8**. What hymn are the creatures chanting? What is the threefold repetition of "holy" a Hebrew way of saying?

For application
1. **4:1.** Eastern Catholic Churches have as many as three doors leading into the sanctuary, and doors form an important part of the Eastern liturgy. What is the symbolism behind a closed door? An open door? Where does this door lead? Look again at 3:20: To what or to whom is the door to your heart open (or closed)?
2. **4:5.** Read the note for this verse. What is the symbolic connection between the Holy Spirit and fire? Why *fire* (as opposed simply to, say, *light*)? Do you have a personal relationship with the Holy Spirit?
3. **4:8.** What is God's holiness? What does his holiness do *to* you? In what ways are you aware of God's holiness?
4. **4:10.** What things does a crown symbolize? Why would the 24 elders cast their crowns (with everything they symbolize) before God's throne? What might that action suggest for your approach to God?

Chapter 5

For understanding
1. **5:1.** What is the scroll? What does it look like? As seen in the subsequent context, what is the role of Christ?
2. **5:5.** What are the OT sources for the messianic titles for Jesus?
3. **5:6.** Though John expects to see a lion, what does he actually see? How many times does this designation for Christ appear in Revelation? How does Christ forever appear, and what does his posture symbolize? What do seven horns and seven eyes represent?
4. **5:9–10.** What does the worship of the Lamb indicate about him? What does the imagery of the song recall? What does it celebrate here?

For application
1. **5:6.** The image of the Lamb standing as though slain upon an altar is a common symbol of the eucharistic liturgy in religious art. How does it communicate the meaning of the Mass? What response does it evoke in you?
2. **5:9–10.** These verses allude to your participation in the kingly and priestly roles of Jesus. At the eucharistic liturgy, how does the priest's role mirror that of Christ? How do we, as the lay faithful, participate in this priestly ministry?
3. **5:11.** If a *myriad* is Greek for the number 10,000, consider the number of angels and saints who join us in worship.What might the sheer quantity of fellow worshipers suggest for your participation in the Mass?
4. **5:12–14.** Of the four principal forms of prayer—adoration, thanksgiving, petition, and repentance—which do you see most often in the Mass? Which do you do most often when you pray privately? If God does not need our worship, why should we worship him?

Chapter 6

For understanding

1. **6:1—8:5.** What does the breaking of the seven seals bring about? What do these seals parallel in Jesus' preaching? What does history tell us about their fulfillment? What relationship do the sevenfold disasters mentioned bear to the Torah? Although devastating, for what are these disasters merely a prelude? In Revelation, for what do they serve as the backdrop?

2. **6:1–8.** When are the four horsemen summoned, and what does each symbolize? From where in the Prophets does this vision come? What message does Revelation communicate by means of these images?

3. **6:9.** To what is the altar mentioned here a heavenly counterpart? Who are those slain for the word? Why do their pleas for justice come from beneath the altar? What is martyrdom thus portrayed as being?

4. **6:17.** Of what is the act of standing a sign? Who assumes this posture in Revelation? About what were Nahum and Malachi warning?

For application

1. **6:1–8.** Read the note for these verses. In what ways are *punishment* and *chastisement* both similar and different? Ideally, what is the purpose of each?

2. **6:9–11.** Why might our age be considered an age of martyrs? If the prospect of sacrificing your life for your faith were to become a reality, what would you do?

3. **6:12–14.** Has your own or your family's life ever been shaken by sudden turns of events? If so, what effects did this have on you, particularly in terms of your faith, your hope, and your love?

4. **6:16–17.** What is the *wrath* of God? If God is Love, as Christians believe, why does Scripture speak—even in the New Testament—of divine wrath?

Chapter 7

For understanding

1. **7:3.** What is the purpose of a seal? Who receives the seal in this vision? With what does the seal of God contrast within the broader context of Revelation? How does the entire scene parallel Ezek 9:1–7?

2. **7:5–8.** What two irregularities stand out in the enumeration of the 12 tribes? What may explain each irregularity? Whatever the precise reason for these irregularities, why was the number kept at 12?

3. **7:9.** Who are in the "great multitude" that John sees? Whom does the uncountable throng represent? For what were palm branches used? What is the OT background for this vision?

4. **Word Study: Shelter (7:15).** What does the Greek word for "to shelter" mean? What memory from the OT inspires its usage? From John's perspective, what function does the Tabernacle serve? How then does Revelation use the verb "to shelter"?

For application

1. **7:2–3.** When you make the sign of the Cross, what are you acknowledging? What is the significance of being sealed with this sign in Confirmation?

2. **7:4–8.** Read the note for v. 4. How many messianic Jews, Jewish Christians, or Hebrew Catholics do you know? What contribution to Christian—especially Catholic—faith do Jewish/Hebrew Christians offer?

3. **7:9–12.** How much time per week do you spend in adoration of God (that is, without asking him for anything)? What can you learn from vv. 10 and 12 about how to offer prayers of adoration?

4. **7:14–17.** Which of the three theological virtues (faith, hope, and love) do these verses describe? What is the focal point of this virtue? How might you gain strength in your practice of this virtue?

Chapter 8

For understanding

1. **8:1.** What kind of silence does the "silence in heaven" recall? Of what other kind of silence does Jewish tradition speak? What, then, is happening in the context of this background?
2. **8:3.** How do the priests on earth resemble angels in heaven? Who comprise the company of all the saints in heaven? What doctrine is the basis for their intercession?
3. **8:7—11:19.** How do the coming seven trumpet blasts compare with what happened with the preceding seven seals? The following seven bowls? On what scriptural events are the first four trumpet blasts modeled?
4. **8:11.** What is wormwood, and what does it symbolize? What is the connection here with the story in Ex 15:22–25?

For application

1. **8:1.** What is the value of silence for prayer? What is the difference between "dead" silence and a living silence? Which better characterizes your experience of prayer?
2. **8:3–4.** What characteristics make incense a good symbol for prayer? According to the note for v. 3, what kind of prayer is being offered here?
3. **8:6.** For what are trumpets used in the Bible? What kind of response do you think they are intended to evoke?

Chapter 9

For understanding

1. **9:1–12.** What happens when the fifth trumpet sounds? What are the warrior locusts? What restrictions are placed on their activity? What do these limitations suggest? How does this plague compare with the vision of the prophet Joel?
2. **9:1.** Of what is the fallen star a traditional image? To what does the "bottomless pit" correspond? In the cosmology of Israel, who dwelt there? How does Christ control this realm?
3. **9:11.** What do the names Abaddon and Apollyon mean in their original languages? With what is Abaddon associated in the OT?
4. **9:13–21.** What force does the sixth trumpet unbind? How are these beasts different in their destructiveness from the locusts?

For application

1. **9:3–6.** What do locusts normally eat? According to John, whom are they supposed to attack? What would have protected them?
2. **9:7–11.** Although the locusts are ferocious in appearance and are led by "the Destroyer", what damage are they allowed to do to the followers of the Lamb (see v. 4)? How is this similar to the authority Satan has over the followers of Jesus?
3. **9:15–19.** If "the wages of sin is death" (Rom 6:23), how does this killing show divine justice? "Since all have sinned and fallen short of the glory of God" (Rom 3:23), what is the source of our hope that we might enter heaven?
4. **9:20–21.** Why do you think the scale of the killing in the previous verses only hardens the hearts of some people? Based on your experience, how common is this reaction?

Chapter 10

For understanding

1. **10:1—11:14.** What is happening between the sixth and seventh trumpet? What does it set in motion? What does it mean for John?
2. **10:1–11.** What does the angel that John sees look like? What does the angel of the Lord do elsewhere in Scripture? How is the Book of Daniel pertinent? What do the similarities between Dan 10–12 and Rev 10 imply about the timetable of the prophecy?
3. **10:7.** What is happening to the "mystery of God"? Where in the OT is the link between the "mystery" and the messianic "kingdom" forged?
4. **10:9.** Why is John told to take and eat the scroll? Why does the message taste sweet but then turn sour? On what other Scripture passage is the scene modeled?

For application

1. **10:4.** If you had to describe to someone else, such as a spiritual director, what is happening in your spiritual life, how easy or hard would it be for you to do this? Why do you think many mystics have such difficulty discussing the content of their experiences?
2. **10:9** What is your own prophetic role as a baptized Christian? What is the balance between sweetness and suffering in your exercise of this role?
3. **10:10.** In order to exercise a prophetic role, what must you first do, according to the first half of this verse? How would you do that?
4. **10:11.** At whose initiative does the prophet perform his ministry? What is the role of vocation (or calling by the Lord) in what you do?

Chapter 11

For understanding

1. **11:1.** Describe the prophetic action that John is asked to perform. What distinction is he told to make, and what is the significance of this? Explain how different interpreters offer different answers to the question: What did John measure? What is the OT background for this symbolic action?
2. **11:2.** Explain two different ways one might read this verse. What is the meaning of the "forty-two months"? From where in the OT is this figure drawn?
3. **Word Study: Witnesses (11:3).** In what four ways is the word "witness" used in the NT and in Christian history? Which of these is the dominant sense in the Book of Revelation?
4. **11:8.** What is the "great city" to which John refers? What are its crimes? What is implied by its comparison to "Sodom" and "Egypt"?
5. **11:15–19.** What happens when the seventh trumpet sounds? What is the twofold biblical backdrop for this event?

For application

1. **11:1.** In colloquial language, what does it mean to "take the measure" of something or someone? By what standard would you take the measure of your spiritual life?
2. **11:3–12.** How would you measure the health of the churches throughout the world that have undergone persecution over the last 75 years or so? What are some examples? Why do you think such churches grow stronger rather than weaker?
3. **11:15.** What are some of the ways in which the expression "kingdom of God" can be understood? How can the existence of this kingdom be at once visible here and now and yet a mystery?
4. **11:19.** What considerations prompted many Church Fathers to link the Ark of the Covenant with Mary? How may the image of the Ark also be applied to the Church? To you yourself?

Chapter 12

For understanding
1. **12:1–6.** What three things does the woman of Rev 12 represent? What is the fourfold biblical background upon which John is drawing in his depiction of this scene?
2. **12:3.** What does the great red dragon represent? What do his horns and his diadems symbolize? For what did this draconic serpent stand in the ancient Near East? What is he called, and how is he pictured?
3. **12:5.** Who is the "male child" that is born? What image connects him with Ps 2? How is this psalm fulfilled in Christ, according to the NT?
4. **12:13–17.** What happens when the devil is slammed down to earth? What does this imagery recall from OT narratives?

For application
1. **12:1.** Read the note for vv. 1–6. Why is the appearance of the woman called a "great sign"? What makes her a sign of Mary? What makes her a sign of the Church?
2. **12:3.** Why is the appearance of the dragon also called a sign? A sign of what?
3. **12:6, 14.** These verses mention the flight of the woman into the wilderness. What is God able to do for his people in the wilderness that is not done anywhere else?
4. **12:17.** Some theologians and spiritual writers speak of "spiritual warfare". What does the term mean to you? How might events in your life indicate that you are engaged in spiritual warfare? How is the Church at large engaged in it?

Chapter 13

For understanding
1. **13:1–2.** In what ways does the beast from the sea mimic the Lamb and assume the posture of a rival? From what OT vision do the animal features of the beast come? What is different about the way the OT and Revelation use this imagery?
2. **13:3.** What do the seven heads of the beast represent? What are two ways of understanding the healing of the beast's mortal wound?
3. **13:17.** What choice does the beast force the world to make? What does the note suggest may be the historical background?
4. **13:18.** Of what is the number *six hundred and sixty-six* probably a cryptogram? Why is the reference to Nero as the beast entirely apt? Where else in the Bible does the number 666 appear, and what is its significance? In light of this, what does the note suggest Solomon may typify?

For application
1. **13:1–2.** Read the note for these verses. What do you think is the "beast" of our day? How does it mimic the role of religious faith?
2. **13:4.** What effects can you see of this "beast" in the world at large? Have you been affected by it? As the verse asks, how can you fight against it?
3. **13:11.** Read the note for this verse. Again, what might this beast be in our time? That is, what in our culture looks innocent but speaks an insidious language that draws its listeners to worship the beast you identified just now?
4. **13:16–17.** Whose "mark" did you receive when you were baptized? Whose sign do you make upon yourself when you pray? How can this mark or sign fight against the authority of the beasts you identified?

Chapter 14

For understanding

1. **14:1.** What does Mount Zion represent here? Of what is the earthly Zion a visible model? In the OT, for what does Zion serve as the focal point? What is its connection with John's vision? What is the significance of the Lamb's name and the Father's name written on the foreheads of those gathered there?
2. **14:4.** What is the literal rendering of "they are chaste"? What two levels of meaning would this expression probably have?
3. **14:8.** Where was Babylon, and for what was it infamous? How does the way the angel speaks of the fall of this city resemble the OT oracles about the fall of Babylon?
4. **14:14–20.** How are the judgments of the righteous and the wicked described? How does the analogy describe what happens to members of both groups? Where else in Scripture do similar scenes of divine judgment appear?

For application

1. **14:4.** Why is chastity such a significant virtue for followers of Jesus? How important is this virtue for you, whether you are married or single?
2. **14:7.** Is God's judgment something for Christians to be afraid of or to hope for? How do you view the prospect that God will sooner or later judge you?
3. **14:13.** Why are the dead who die in the Lord blessed? What did judgment mean for them? Why is it appropriate to pray for their intercession?
4. **14:14–20.** Why is it appropriate that judgment should begin with the People of God? In the context of the note for these verses, what do the verses themselves indicate may be the outcome of that judgment?

Chapter 15

For understanding

1. **15:2–4.** What does John see and hear as a prelude to judgment? What song is being sung? What was the original song about, and how are the martyrs adapting it?
2. **15:6.** What is the significance of the bright linen? Why do the angels wear golden sashes?
3. **15:7** What are the golden bowls? What idea is reinforced by the use of these bowls to pour out plagues?
4. **15:8.** What is cutting off access to the throne room? What three OT events does it recall?

For application

1. **15:3a.** Why is *singing* an appropriate response to victory? How does singing sometimes enhance the experience of prayer?
2. **15:3b–4.** If God does not need our praise, why do we praise him? How are these verses a good model for a prayer of praise?
3. **15:6.** What is the main function of an angel? Why would these angels be dressed as Levitical priests? What do angelic and priestly functions have to do with your role as a baptized Christian in the world?
4. **15:8.** What does the term *glory* mean in ordinary usage? When applied to God? If entering into that glory is your final destiny, why should God hide it from you now?

Chapter 16

For understanding
1. **16:1–21.** How is the emptying of the seven bowls of wrath unlike the cycle of the seven seals and the seven trumpets? On which of the Exodus plagues are five of the seven bowls modeled?
2. **16:12.** Where is the river Euphrates? What is its connection with earlier biblical history?
3. **16:16.** What does the word *Armageddon* mean? What was its historical location, and how was that location used? What is Revelation ultimately envisioning? What memories of victory and defeat does the plain of Megiddo evoke?
4. **16:21.** What does the final bowl bring upon the wicked Babylon?

For application
1. **16:1–21.** What spiritual response do you make to news of wars, earthquakes and other natural disasters, and economic privation all over the world? What spiritual responsibility do you have for them?
2. **16:5–7.** When is rejoicing at the overthrow of the wicked appropriate for a Christian? How might such rejoicing be inappropriate?
3. **16:8–9.** If you are a parent, how do you encourage your children to repent through the punishments you administer? What do you do if the children refuse to repent?
4. **16:18.** Have you ever experienced an earthquake? Why is an earthquake so terrifying? On a spiritual level, what might an earthquake symbolize for you, and what effects might it have on your relationship with God?

Chapter 17

For understanding
1. **Topical Essay: Who Is Babylon?** How have interpreters identified the "Babylon" of Revelation? What are some of the arguments in favor of the two positions? Is it possible to hold that both are legitimate interpretations?
2. **17:1.** What does the recurring verb *seated* symbolize in this vision? It points to a relationship between what two historical entities? What is the symbolism of "many waters"? What is the connection with ancient Babylon?
3. **17:9.** The image of seven hills leads many to identify the harlot of Revelation with what ancient city? According to the note, how does an examination of the symbolism open the way for a different interpretation?
4. **17:10.** List some possible interpretations of the "seven kings". Read literally, who are possible candidates for being the sixth king? Whom do ancient historians normally identify as Rome's first king?

For application
1. **17:1–6.** Read the note for v. 1. How many meanings can you think of for the verb *to sit* (or, alternatively, *to seat*)? Why do you think John places such emphasis on the harlot's being seated?
2. **17:9.** Read the note for this verse, considering again the harlot's position. How does it indicate *alliance*? How does this image apply to the position many of us take with respect to the world?
3. **17:12–14.** Think of the totalitarian regimes of the 20th century (e.g., Communist Russia, Nazi Germany, Idi Amin's Uganda, and others). On what were they seated? How does the "one hour" of authority apply to them? With respect to the saints, what do they all have in common?

Chapter 18

For understanding

1. **18:1–24.** What is happening in these verses? What images in this chapter are taken from the judgment oracles of the Prophets?
2. **18:4.** In what two ways has the call to "come out of her" been interpreted? What NT passages are used to support these different readings? What plagues are being referred to in this verse?
3. **18:9–19.** Who are the representative clients of the harlot? Why are they saddened at her destruction? From where is this subsection of the chapter drawn?

For application

1. **18:4–5.** Because you live in the world and must have dealings with it, what are some of the dangers to faith as you engage in political and economic activities? For example, how seriously do you take the Church's admonition not to engage in unnecessary work—including commercial activity—on the Lord's day (see CCC 2185)?
2. **18:9–10.** According to the *Catechism* (CCC 1882, 2239, 2442), what involvement should Catholics have in the political process? What are some of the benefits and dangers of this involvement?
3. **18:11–17a.** Why have recent popes criticized the capitalist system for its outlook on world markets? What is the capitalist view of making a profit? How does this view square with the Christian perspective (see CCC 2426–42)?
4. **18:17b–19.** According to Catholic social teaching, to whom do the material goods of the world belong (see CCC 2402–6, 2437–49)? What is the responsibility of rich nations like ours for the welfare of poorer nations?

Chapter 19

For understanding

1. **Word Study: Hallelujah (19:1, 3, 4, 6).** Of what is this word a transliteration? How many times does it appear in the NT? How is it used in the Psalms? What do some scholars maintain is the background of the repeated "Hallelujah" in Rev 19? To what does it build up? What does the word have to do with the celebration of the Christian Eucharist?
2. **19:7–9.** What are these verses describing? How does John envision the Church? How is she dressed? What does the marriage of the bridal city recall in Ezekiel?
3. **19:11–16.** How does Christ appear in these verses? What is his mission? What does the depiction of Christ dressed in a blood-covered robe and treading the winepress of wrath recall? What does the depiction of him as the Word swinging a sharp sword recall?
4. **19:17–21.** Describe what is going on in these verses. What kind of judgment is envisioned? According to the note, what historical happenings may be linked to the condemnation of the "beast" and the "false prophet"? From where does the vision of "the great supper" come?

For application

1. **19:5.** What role does praise of God play in your prayer life? Why is praise commanded here?
2. **19:11–13.** Why is Jesus depicted here as a fierce warrior rather than the Prince of Peace? In spite of the discomfort that many moderns have with military imagery, how might it be appropriate in Catholic spirituality?
3. **19:9.** Who *is* invited to the "marriage supper of the Lamb"? What is your role in ensuring that the invitation is accepted?
4. **19:15.** Why does a sharp sword come out of Christ's *mouth*? What does it symbolize? Why a sword?

Chapter 20

For understanding

1. **20:1–6.** Explain the three main ways that theologians have interpreted the millennium of Rev 20. What has been the most widely held view, historically speaking? What does the note suggest as the OT background for the millennium? What is the Catholic Church's official position on this question?
2. **20:5.** What are two possible ways of understanding the first and second resurrection in Revelation? What are some other NT passages that lend support to these views?
3. **20:8.** Who are Gog and Magog? From where do these names come? What happens to them?
4. **20:11–15.** What is the Last Judgment? What happens during it? What is the outcome of that day?

For application

1. **20:1–6.** Read the note for these verses. Of the interpretations of the millennium surveyed, which do you think is most likely? Why do you think the Church rejects millenarianism?
2. **20:6.** Assuming the "first death" is physical death, what does the note for this verse say the term "second death" means? What does the *Catechism* say about it (CCC 1033–37)?
3. **20:10.** Why would a loving God create a place or state of eternal torment? Why does he allow people to go there?
4. **20:13.** On what basis are we judged? What part do motives play in how we are judged?

Chapter 21

For understanding

1. **21:1.** What does it mean to say there will be a "new heaven" and a "new earth"? In what way does this involve a process of regeneration? From where does this imagery come? What does it mean for the sea to cease to exist?
2. **21:2.** What is the new Jerusalem? Why does the new Jerusalem touch down to earth? To what city, described earlier in the book, is the heavenly Jerusalem the antithesis? What suggests this?
3. **21:9–22:5.** With what do these verses deal? From where do the details of this vision come, and what are they? Where else in Scripture are there visions of Jerusalem adorned in this way?
4. **21:16.** What shape does the eternal city have? What may have served as the model for this shape?

For application

1. **21:1.** Read the note for this verse. Based on what you already know about the symbolism of the earth and the sea in Revelation, what might John regard as a new heaven and a new earth? What, for example, does worship have to do with it?
2. **21:3–7.** How does God dwell with men already? What will be the difference between how he dwells with us now and how he will dwell with us in the way described in John's vision? How might you increase your desire to have God live with you?
3. **21:8.** With what kinds of people does God refuse to dwell? What is it about their behavior (especially habitual behavior) that God finds repugnant?
4. **21:22–25.** What is the source of light for the heavenly city? Since a baptized Christian is a temple of the Holy Spirit, what should be the source of his light even in this life? How would you recognize it when you see it?

Chapter 22

For understanding

1. **22:1.** Of what is the "water of life" symbolic? To what does this imagery allude? How is the water an apocalyptic expression of a trinitarian mystery?
2. **22:2.** Other than in the present verse, where did the "tree of life" make an appearance in the Bible? What might its reappearance here be intended to convey?
3. **22:4.** What is the great hope of biblical spirituality? What does tradition call it? To what does it point?
4. **22:10.** What is John commanded not to do? Why is reading John's message a top priority for his churches? How is this command in contrast to Dan 12:4?
5. **22:18–19.** What warning is given here? What similar warning did Moses give?

For application

1. **22:1–2.** Where does the river of life (the Holy Spirit) flow? To what does it give life? What purpose do the leaves of the tree of life serve? How does all this imagery apply to the Holy Spirit in your life?
2. **22:4.** What does "seeing the face" of someone mean? In this life, Scripture urges us to "seek the face" of God. How might you do that? What should the results of seeking God's face be?
3. **22:13.** What does this verse suggest about the meaning of life? Regardless of your background, your career, your state in life, or your plans for the future, what does it all come to in the end?
4. **22:17.** A saying in the software industry goes, "If you have a good product, and nobody buys it, raise the price." Is the Holy Spirit free or priceless? How much will possession of the Holy Spirit cost you?

BOOKS OF THE BIBLE

THE OLD TESTAMENT (OT)

Gen	Genesis
Ex	Exodus
Lev	Leviticus
Num	Numbers
Deut	Deuteronomy
Josh	Joshua
Judg	Judges
Ruth	Ruth
1 Sam	1 Samuel
2 Sam	2 Samuel
1 Kings	1 Kings
2 Kings	2 Kings
1 Chron	1 Chronicles
2 Chron	2 Chronicles
Ezra	Ezra
Neh	Nehemiah
Tob	Tobit
Jud	Judith
Esther	Esther
Job	Job
Ps	Psalms
Prov	Proverbs
Eccles	Ecclesiastes
Song	Song of Solomon
Wis	Wisdom
Sir	Sirach (Ecclesiasticus)
Is	Isaiah
Jer	Jeremiah
Lam	Lamentations
Bar	Baruch
Ezek	Ezekiel
Dan	Daniel
Hos	Hosea
Joel	Joel
Amos	Amos
Obad	Obadiah
Jon	Jonah
Mic	Micah
Nahum	Nahum
Hab	Habakkuk
Zeph	Zephaniah
Hag	Haggai
Zech	Zechariah
Mal	Malachi
1 Mac	1 Maccabees
2 Mac	2 Maccabees

THE NEW TESTAMENT (NT)

Mt	Matthew
Mk	Mark
Lk	Luke
Jn	John
Acts	Acts of the Apostles
Rom	Romans
1 Cor	1 Corinthians
2 Cor	2 Corinthians
Gal	Galatians
Eph	Ephesians
Phil	Philippians
Col	Colossians
1 Thess	1 Thessalonians
2 Thess	2 Thessalonians
1 Tim	1 Timothy
2 Tim	2 Timothy
Tit	Titus
Philem	Philemon
Heb	Hebrews
Jas	James
1 Pet	1 Peter
2 Pet	2 Peter
1 Jn	1 John
2 Jn	2 John
3 Jn	3 John
Jude	Jude
Rev	Revelation (Apocalypse)